Rhythms of Renewal

Letitia Suk

This JOY!
Elgin, Illinois

Rhythms of Renewal by Letitia Suk
Published by This Joy! Books
P.O. Box 823
Elgin, IL 60121
A division of Three Cord Ministries, Inc.
Milwaukee Avenue, Libertyville, IL
thisjoybooks@gmail.com

Cover design by Gretchen Stibolt.

Author photo by Jennifer Schuman of Horizon Photography.

Art on the cover is an original watercolor by Judith Hollister at judithhollistergallery.com

Printed in the United States of America

To Tom

❧

The Best is Yet to Be

Acknowledgments

❧ There are so many who have been a part of my journey to bring this book to life. I am especially grateful for:

❧ My husband, Tom, and our family, Jeshua and Jessica, Gabriel, Selah, and Christa who inspire me daily to live my own abundant life.

❧ My mother, Betty Wiewel, who has loved me the longest.

❧ My women's group of Marge Carhart, Theresa Decker, Barb Horowitz, Cindy Nicholson, and Sue Swidryk who prayed for this project all the way through.

❧ The inspiration and encouragement of Jane Rubietta.

❧ Special thanks to Ginny Emery who brought it all together in a most amazing way. Her team includes Lillian McAnally, Gretchen Stibolt, and Judith Hollister.

❧ I also give thanks to Jesus, the one who said, "I came so they can have real and eternal life, more and better life than they ever dreamed of" (John 10:10, MSG).

Table of Contents

Welcome to Something New!

According to *Merriam-Webster's Online Dictionary*, *renewal* means, "to make like new; restore to freshness, vigor, or perfection; to make new spiritually; to begin again." What a delicious definition! Should we all line up for a refill? The culture seems to think so. A quick glance at bestseller lists indicates quite a bit of renewal going around if all the self-help books purchased are actually read. The latest editions of glossy women's magazines proclaim *new* styles, *new* ways to communicate, *new* health trends, and *new* Hollywood stars to watch. Department stores across the world lure customers with the promise of *new* colors for this season and even grocery stores are well stocked with *new* and improved items. (Which, if you think about it, is somewhat of an oxymoron: how can something be new *and* improved? Obviously, if it's new, it's not an improvement from a previous version.)

The idea of renewing our self-image tantalizes us to search for the latest hairstyle as we cut it, grow it, color it, perm it, and straighten it. We embrace new diets that promise the hope of a new body by just eating no carbs, more carbs, and back around again.

The idea of renewal spills over into our homes as we seek to redecorate, whether it's changing the wall color, new window treatments, or at least rearrange the furniture. In the kitchen, renewal comes in the form of cookbooks that sell promises for new recipes with delicious flavors, time saved, family mealtime fun, *and* improved health benefits.

The problem is that new things don't stay new. What we still call the new couch in our home is about twelve years old, new shoes soon need to be replaced, new cars need repairs, and new clothes become worn. That's where the *re*-new comes in: make it like new all over again. We do this repeatedly as we replace, recover, restock, and rearrange.

As Ecclesiastes 1:9 states, "There is nothing new under the sun." True, but we become quite adept at reshaping the old to look like new. Why? Because, with change, we come alive; it is something that God has coded into our beings. We are wired for renewal.

Our spiritual journeys reflect our high need for renewal as well. It is exciting to connect with God in a life-changing way. Prayer flows from our hearts, Bible verses jump off the page, all the doors we have knocked on seem to open all around us—until prayer seems dry, Bible reading seems boring, and we can't recall a time recently when we really felt God's presence. Sound familiar?

Renewal from the inside out is God's agenda for *all* of our lives, not just the hidden parts. What He starts in our hearts, He wants to finish in our homes. We often quickly settle for renewal *á la carte* instead of trusting God to transform every area of our lives.

Our God cares about every moment we live each day. This book is about life-shaping rhythms of renewal that will extend from our heart to our kitchen, workplace, and everything else in between that we come in contact with.

Practical Guide to Renewal

Each chapter of this book focuses on a different aspect of renewal for women. To make the most of each topic, I've included three sections at the end of each chapter—*Response,*

The Small Group Speaks, and *Rituals of Renewal*—to help you weave into your heart and life what you have read.

The *Response* section offers reflective questions to take you deeper into the material. Next, *The Small Group Speaks* is a section where other women in an anecdotal setting share their thoughts and experience on the chapter's topic. *Rhythms of Renewal* is written for all women who want to experience more of the fullness of life God has planned for us. To help you connect with the concepts, I invited seven women who are in different seasons of life to participate in the writing by sharing their stories.

- *Deb Davis,* 49, mother of six and grandmother of one, teacher
- *Glenna Ganster,* 55, mom of two adult daughters and one college-age son, Bible study teacher and psychotherapist
- *Sandy Garrison,* 42, mother of one, antique dealer
- *Kristy Hamilton,* 47, mother of four, social worker
- *Linda Jones,* 56, single mom to three grown daughters, administrative assistant
- *Eloise McDowell,* 62, married for the first time at 61, children's pastor
- *Tara Montgomery,* 36, stay-at-home mom to two young boys, private reading tutor

Finally, I offer practical suggestions for enriching your life, which I call, *Rituals of Renewal.*

Ladies, we are all on a spiritual journey. Renewal is about letting God take you to the next place. Some of you have been on this journey for a long time and sometimes wonder if there is anything new to see. Some of you are in such a hurry to get to the next place that you might miss out on some of the finer points of the trip. Some of you aren't even sure if you've signed up yet, but come along for the ride.

God has a plan for renewal for you that is for the here and now—not for the elusive next phase of your life. As women we are good at hearing with the heart. Start by being open to the touch of the Father in new ways, ask Him to reveal Himself to you. Come along.

Renewal . . . how I would like that in my closet! What did I wear last fall anyway? There is nothing here that is not white or wool. Renewal . . . I'll take a box of that in my kitchen. This oregano is about three years old, my wedding dishes are chipped, and why don't they give you 20th anniversary showers when you really need new stuff? Renewal . . . I think we're having a meeting about it at church, but I have to be at my son's basketball game that night. Renewal . . . wait a minute, it's not New Year's yet!

Chapter One

Renewal

Like most women, I like something new! I have been known to rearrange an entire room to showcase a new item that I purchased at a garage sale. One magazine article can set me designing a whole new day-to-day schedule. Buying a new sweater can lead to an afternoon of sorting out the closet to discover what pants and skirts go with it.

Ladies, since we are wired to receive and experience new things, boredom quickly catches our attention. We get bored with our hair, tired of our clothes, disinterested in household chores, ho-hum about our jobs; we coast along. This is normal! Without boredom, we would not be motivated to change.

The same is true of our spiritual practices, only we hesitate to call them boring because that doesn't seem right. Noticing our prayers are sounding more like grocery lists than communication with the Creator of the universe is often an early sign. Re-reading the same portion of Scripture because we forgot that we just read it, or nodding off instead of listening for the voice of God's direction are indications that a fresh wave of renewal is sorely needed.

Like every other area of our lives, our spiritual lives are in constant need of renewal. Just as we re-design an outfit with a new scarf or a table with candles and flowers, we renew our spiritual practices by trying something *new*.

God's handbook to life, the Bible, has a lot to say about renewal: "Therefore, we do not lose heart. Though outwardly we are wasting away [*ouch, that is blunt, and by the way, where did I leave my reading glasses?*], yet inwardly we are being renewed day by day" *(*2 Cor. 4:16). Renewal is ongoing because of God's Spirit within us. When we position ourselves for something new by cooperating, making room for it, the process speeds up.

What Are You Growing in Your Garden?

I am a fantasy gardener. Every February I fantasize about what my garden will look like the following summer. Nothing is out of the range of possibility in the winter when the only work to do is to imagine. Yet, each spring some extenuating circumstance jumps up that keeps me from designing, shopping for, or even planting the garden of my dreams. By July I usually have some small seedlings in the ground and decide that next year I'll start planting earlier. Meanwhile, I'm still growing tomatoes in late October!

If you have ever gardened, you remember clearing the ground, planting, watering, fertilizing, and pulling weeds long before you get to enjoy the fruits of your labor. We are caretakers, the gardeners if you wish, of our lives. It is a two-part deal. We position ourselves for spiritual renewal (the watering, fertilizing, pulling weeds part), and God does the renewing as we are transformed to His likeness (growing and harvesting).

God can certainly get our attention in a myriad of fashions. We can position our hearts for renewal first by showing up and asking for it. Most of us have probably had an ah-ha moment in the shower, in the car, or at the kitchen sink. I love those moments when God invades the ordinary and the answer or direction I have been seeking is staring me in the face.

But most of the time, however, my relationship with God is cultivated and deepened the same way my relationship with anyone else is—by putting in the time, giving God the chance to speak, and then listening to the still small voice of the Lord whispering to my heart and following through by doing what He tells me to do. (See Isaiah 30:21.)

Seasons of Life

Over the years, I have learned that there are many seasons to life and "There is a time for everything and a season for every activity under heaven" (Eccls. 3:1) is the story of all of our lives. Life is in a state of flux most of the time; *you* become the constant. Your season of life will change with the time of the year, the time of the month, the ages and needs of your children, the issues facing your husband or extended family, where you are in your career, and even with the weather.

Renewal fits your season of life. If you are a mother of young children, you can count on that "He gently leads those that have young" (Isa. 40:11). Something new for you might include opportunities to connect with God while you're caring for your child. As you bathe your baby, ask that you both be kept clean from sin. As you feed your toddler, ask to be fed with the bread of life. Perhaps you could listen to worship music as you drive the car pool. Use part of the time your little ones nap to read the Bible and connect with God. Ask Him to show you new places where He is waiting for you.

If you're a working girl (and who isn't!), spiritual renewal might involve listening to the Gospels on your mp3 player while you commute to work or reading a few pages of an inspiring book over your lunch. Consider also finding or starting a Bible or book study at your place of work. Groups that meet regularly for prayer or study over lunch or after hours can be frequently found in urban areas.

Often God will renew you as you reach out to your co-workers in new and creative ways. Looking for ways to serve, being available to listen, offering to pray for their tough situations can take you to a whole new place in your relationship to God as you watch Him work in the lives of others.

Spiritual renewal can be like shopping for new clothes. How does this fit? Does this belt go with this skirt? What color jacket would look good with this? Like choosing a new accessory to go with a familiar outfit, new ways of connecting with God often build on a foundation that's already there. Life-giving practices of prayer and time in the Word have sustained me for many years; they are an essential part of who I am. Through many seasons of life, being single, married without kids, mother of many small children, and now an empty nester, continuity in these practices has grounded me. These disciplines have stood the test of time and varied circumstances although the details change from season to season.

A Basket of Books

I am a morning girl. I love being up alone in the house before the phone rings and errands start calling. My first stop is the kitchen where the teakettle waits for me. While it is heating up, I make a quick stop at the computer to see if my late-night college kids have sent any news flashes. Then it's tea in the mug to brew, English muffin in the toaster, and off to the shower. After my shower, I head back to the kitchen to gather the tea and muffin and off to the living room to *my* chair.

Beside my chair is a basket laden with an assortment of books. First volume out is my daily list of what I'm grateful for, five things every day albeit the mundane, the silly, the exciting, the relieving. Just five things because it is time to move on. The next book that comes out is my daily family journal (more about that in chapter four) where I write a paragraph or less on what happened the previous day.

Next comes a devotional book, which might be a year-long set of reflections or a book that is particularly inspiring and challenging to me right now. Then out of the basket comes my Bible and current study guide or reading guide (more detail to come later). Finally, I take out my prayer journal and begin my daily prayers for my family and other concerns. I finish by writing what's on my heart in the form of prayers. All in all, it takes about half an hour. Without this ritual, I'm not ready for the day.

When I was young and single, I prayed, read, and wrote in my journal late at night. When my children were babies and I was up in the middle of the night to care for them, that slot became my time to connect with God. There was no basket then! During the stage when they were small and everywhere, I would pray during educational children's TV! They usually wanted me in the same room, but it wasn't hard to tune out Oscar the Grouch and tune into God. It was a good plan for that season of my life.

As soon as they were all in school, it was easier to connect with God as soon as the last one left the house, but don't school kids have a LOT of days off?

Now the time is all mine again as they wake up in their dormitories and apartments and get themselves off, so I'm back to meeting God first thing in the morning.

Take a Look Behind You

Sometimes renewal starts with looking back. The word to the church at Ephesus in Revelation 2:5 was to "repent and do the things you did at first." What practices were part of *your* early relationship with Jesus?

I made the decision to follow Jesus while I was in college. Although my parents had brought me up in a church and I knew a lot about religion, I didn't have much of an intimate relationship with God. I spent my late teens free-floating spiritually until one day in Colorado, in the summer of 1970, when I was confronted by the truth of Jesus' life and death. I realized there was no room to sit on the fence and I needed to choose to get in or out. I made the choice to let go of doing things my way and to give myself over to the One who created me, who knew me and loved me more than anyone else. When I reached the end of my rope and took hold of Jesus' hand, I was changed forever.

The things I did at first included reading the New Testament like the latest best-selling novel. I looked forward to all-night prayer meetings with my new Christian friends, and I used my lunch hour to memorize portions of Scripture while sitting in the stairwell to avoid office chatter. Fasting a meal once a week and using the dinner hour to listen to Biblical tapes (I know this dates me!) was a treat. I loved doing all these things because I was so in love in Jesus.

What were the early seasons of your spiritual walk like? Did you experience early intimacy? If so, going back to spiritual beginnings can be like going on a second honeymoon with Jesus. We rekindle what has been there all along.

Renewal can also be triggered by asking yourself questions.
What time of the day is it easiest for me to engage in communion with the Lord?
Do I want to have something to eat or drink while I'm praying—"Tea time with Jesus?"
What do I really want to be focusing on in prayer right now?
Do I pray better with lists or as the Spirit leads?
What do I really want to pray for my kids?

Sometimes finding a new prayer style can do wonders. One that has been around for a long time because it works is the *ACTS* plan.

Adore God with your words or songs.

Confess your sins—anything that stands between you and Him.

Thankfulness—remember to be thankful in all situations.

Supplication, which is a fancy word for asking. It encompasses all the stuff we need God's help with.

Even small external changes can nurture renewal. Change the lighting in your prayer area by replacing a cool light bulb with a warm one. Find a small pillow for the small of your back. Crazy as this sounds, a while back I realized I didn't care for the style of my Bible. I bought one in the style and the color I liked and I was so excited to open it! Was it the color that brought it more alive? *No*, but the newness factor really helped.

With sixty-six books in the Bible, reading it from cover-to-cover can seem overwhelming. Daily reading plans break the whole book down into day-size portions. Many are available or you could design your own plan. Special Bibles can be purchased that have it all sorted for you, if that's your preference. For digging deeper, Bible study plans are available for a myriad of topics and range from "fill in the blank" to a more reflective meditation style.

For a fresh perspective, try picking up a classic inspirational devotional like Oswald Chamber's works or inspiring books from authors such as Madeleine L'Engle, C. S. Lewis, John Eldredge or Beth Moore. Browsing online or brick and mortar bookstores will yield many possibilities.

When we are open to the touch of the Father in new ways, He will not disappoint us. Lamentations 3 is one of the most impassioned portions of Scripture. After the author anguishes about affliction, darkness, being walled in, having his heart pierced, his teeth broken, and being trampled in the dust, he concludes with "his compassions never fail. They are new every morning; great is your faithfulness" (vv. 22-23). This man knows renewal.

Renewal involves time alone with God, which takes just that—*time*; time for praying, reading, and the challenging task of waiting on God. Jesus wants your all and, like everything else, your all depends on your season of life. We don't have a "one-size-fits-most" God and He will speak to each of us exactly where we are *now*. Count on it to change. Plan to change with it.

Response

What spiritual practices have been life-giving over the years?

What is one spiritual area that I know needs renewing?

What is the next step I need to follow?

The Small Group Speaks

What does renewal look like in your life?

Sandy: God usually speaks to me through what I'm reading. It's like God gives me a new puzzle piece and then everything is strongly different. Scripture comes alive, prayer feels energized, worship is intimate, and relationships are heightened. It does seem to be seasonal, not necessarily yearly, or even monthly. I've been in a season now for eighteen months; that's probably the longest ever.

Eloise: Renewal is more of a sense of God's presence. I'm usually in a state of peace and rest, hearing from God is clearer, and almost anything I do seems to be blessed. This happens maybe every six weeks or so. It has to do with how rushed my schedule is; the slower the pace, the more frequently I have renewal.

Kristy: Spiritual renewal in my life often shows itself in more personal discipline in areas of my life, such as my conversation, prayer life, and attitude changes. It happens as often as I am willing to give up my stubbornness, listen to what He has for me and stop trying to control every move, even if for a short time.

Linda: First of all, the longing in my heart to spend time with Him becomes stronger until I finally make the time. It is His Spirit calling out to my spirit that draws me to Him, to step into His presence and step away from my world, for a time.

Rituals of Renewal

- Pick out a new pen with your favorite color ink.
- Get a new Bible.
- Find an inspirational book.
- Choose a special mug for use only at your quiet time.
- Design a personalized prayer notebook.
- Update your prayer lists.
- Use photos when praying for family or close friends.
- Organize your prayers by days of the week.
- Read a Proverb each day.
- Listen to worship music while you pray or drive.
- Allow five minutes to just listen to God.
- Write your prayers.
- Use ACTS as a prayer method.
- Keep track of answered prayer.
- Find a new Bible study guide.
- Trade prayers with a friend.
- Fast part of each week.
- Walk as you pray.
- Arrange a prayer corner or area in your home.
- Keep your stuff in a pretty basket.

Repentance . . . Why does that word sound so threatening? This has never been on my top-ten list of fun things to do. Repentance . . . Isn't there a song that goes along with this? Shouldn't I be wearing sackcloth? Repentance . . . I think my pastor talked about this once, but I might have been in the nursery. Repentance . . . I said I was sorry, isn't that good enough?

Chapter Two

Repentance

My college-aged daughter painted her room a lovely shade of green. She rearranged her pictures and mementos on her freshly painted walls and took pains to keep the rest of her room clean (usually!) As long as no one looked at the carpet, her room looked great. The formerly 'beige-colored' carpet, however, had been in her room since before she was born and was now more of a 'tannish' color with dark-brown spots. As beautiful as the rest of her room had become, the carpet was an eyesore.

At last the budget was ready, the time was right, and the new carpet was ordered, but before it could be put down, the old one had to get torn out. Likewise, old wallpaper needs to get stripped off before the new paint will stick. The old couch gets moved out of the room when the new one gets delivered. Jesus referred to this process in several places in the Gospels where he talked about, "no one pours new wine into old wineskins."

When God moves into our hearts in new ways, cleaning out our 'houses' is part of the process. Every time I slip into a heightened sense of God's presence, a clearer perception of His voice speaking into my life, an awareness of His activity all around me, I think it will last forever...*Finally I get it!* From here on out, it's going be you and me God—and nothing will ever come between us.

That is, until my undealt with stuff creeps out of the cubbies of my heart where I've crammed it in and slammed the door. Just like old tires buried in landfills across the country, sooner or later pop up from the ground, my next go-round with God becomes obvious as He gives me the grace to keep digging. It is time to go deeper again.

This is the next step of renewal: *repentance*—a changing of your heart, letting go of whatever is keeping you distant from God, admitting you were wrong after all. Maybe not as fun as getting a new Bible or designing a prayer journal, but certainly very liberating.

Something's Not Right!

The kitchen in our circa 1920 house includes an old-fashioned pantry. It houses the usual mix of seldom-used cookware, seasonal dishes, cans, boxes, and potatoes in a bin in the back. From time to time one of the potatoes starts to rot, sometimes quite obviously! Of course, we usually don't know it right away. A whiff of something peculiar hits the nose upon entry, but it is easily dismissed . . . at first. A few days later the stench permeates the entire tiny room and an excavation ensues. Often the results yield a single rotten potato. When removed from the bin, sweetness returns.

Our sins are like that potato. In the midst of a perfectly normal day (whatever that is!) a sense that something is out of order invades our thoughts of what we're having for dinner. A whiff indicating that all is not quite right with the world creeps in while driving the car pool. We decide that we're just tired and try to catch an extra hour of sleep, but the 'odor' doesn't go away! The urge to go shopping might hit next, followed by browsing the Internet for weekend get-away places. Still, the nagging feeling remains.

The passionate King David put it like this: "When I kept silent, my bones wasted away" (Ps. 32:3). At my mid-life age, there is a slight chance that my bones might be wasting away, but I don't think that is what David is referring to! Sin—both what we have done and what we have failed to do—is not good at keeping silent.

Repentance is cleaning your soul when you know something is rotting; it's living with a clean slate. Often, it is a single issue, an unrepentant area in the midst of an otherwise clean life. Like the potato, sin will continue to fester and increase in odor until we deal with it. What works well in our kitchens applies to our hearts; clean as you go.

Why do we often find cleaning out our hearts so difficult? Sometimes I would rather clean my garage than clean my heart. Too often I lack the courage to pray as David did, "Search me, O God and know my heart; test me and know my anxious thoughts. See if there is any offensive way in me, and lead me in the way everlasting" (Ps. 139:23-24). Like the kid who would rather not open his report card, I don't always want to look at my heart . . . *I'm just fine, thank you. No need to check today . . . oh THAT! Don't worry about THAT, I didn't really mean it . . . oh, that really wasn't a big deal either. Hey, have you checked out HER heart lately?*

My dialogue, or perhaps it's a monologue, tries hard to keep space between my God and me when I don't feel very repentant. *Can you relate to any of this, ladies?*

I don't know about you, but in my times of soul-searching I often find that it is not new issues that play tag with me, but the old ones have returned in colorful camouflage. The same envy that gripped me at sixteen as I coveted my classmate's hair, clothes, or room decor shows up again at fifty, this time longing after designer labels, newer cars, or long vacations. The impatience I felt towards my mother, as she just didn't understand anything, is now aimed at my kids when a veil comes down between our worlds. The titillation of illicit sexual images still lurks, only now it is right out in the open in the magazine pages at the grocery store or on the computer in my family room.

If the same struggles keep popping up, could it be that they were never really dealt with the first time around? Maybe. Sometimes we can fake being sorry just to get God "off our backs," as if He were hounding us in the first place! Instead, He will back off if that's what we want. In His loving insistence, God never forces Himself or His ways on us.

It's more likely, however, that a new level of truth is coming into our beings and we see deeper than we did before. The old sin had been repented of but this new angle on the issue must be dealt with also. *What does this look like?*

As a teenager I sometimes pried loopholes into my parent's rules at my convenience. They said, "Don't see this person tonight." So I saw him the next night even though they meant, "Don't see him tonight or any time." The specific incidents, and there were many, were repented for. However, I also needed to repent of my rebellious attitudes that led me into that behavior. That was a new angle pointed out to me by the Holy Spirit when I was ready to deal with it at a later time. Does that cheapen my previous repentance? No, it affirms the prior repentance by taking it a step deeper.

David prayed, "Test me, O Lord, and try me; examine my heart and mind, for your love is ever before me, and I walk continually in your truth" (Ps. 26:2-3). It is that *love* that allows us to walk in the truth. Repentance keeps the garden of our souls clear of weeds. It is living in freedom.

Once we have truly repented—not like the compulsive "I'm sorry" that my children rapidly spewed from their mouths so they could have their privileges reinstated—it is complete. In Jesus' own words from the cross, "It is finished!" He said those words just as He died for our sins so that we could be clean before God. It is a done deal. *Stop!* Let that sink in.

Sometimes our compulsive natures are uncomfortable with that. It seems too easy, so we try to call unclean what God has made clean (Acts 11:9). I know God forgave me, but I still feel so guilty. We put on our figurative sackcloth and ashes, design penance for ourselves, and settle in for a life of chronic regret. We sink into the bondage again.

Sometimes we are harder on ourselves than God ever is. "Godly sorrow brings repentance that leads to salvation and leaves *no* regret" (2 Cor. 7:10, emphasis added). We finally realize (again) that "The Lord is the Spirit and where the Spirit of the Lord is, there is freedom" (2 Cor. 3:17). It is the taste of that freedom that keeps us coming back to repentance.

The Blameless Life

Our call, as women of God, is to be blameless. Over thirty verses refer to this quality of life. A blameless life is not a sinless life but a forgiven one. Big difference! A finger cannot be pointed because our hearts are clean. This is the quality that set Zechariah and Elizabeth apart, the first character trait of Job to be extolled, the one from whom, no good thing is withheld (Ps. 84:11).

Just as renewal leads to repentance, repentance opens up blameless living. Unlike the sinless life, living blameless is within our reach. We stay blameless by repenting as we go, like keeping up with the cleaning, not allowing for stuff to build up.

Have you ever accidentally bumped against a car and tripped the alarm? The screeching noise is ear piercing! God has created each of us with an internal alarm that can screech to our spirits announcing that a sin invasion is about to happen. He alerts us with this spiritual alarm when anxiety, anger, envy, lust, or judgments want to come in and make themselves at home. Our alarms are individually programmed to go off for the situations that trigger sin in us. Living the blameless life is responding to the alarm.

My alarm for undue anxiety about my kids or my checkbook often goes off way too soon. I think I am doing what any mom does when I wonder what's going on at school, at the neighbors, or at the party on the weekend. Sometimes, I don't just wonder about it though, I obsess over it. The *what-if's* pile up faster than summer flies on spilled lemonade. Likewise, when a big bill is due, my anxiety can overflow like a stopped up sink before I've even had a chance to pray and go over the budget. Some days it feels like I haven't even begun to understand what Paul means when he says "Do not be anxious about anything" (Phil. 1:6) and I wonder how well he would have done if he had kids!

I do know, however, that anxiety will suffocate God's work, so when the alarm goes off, I try to pay attention.

When we walk the blameless path, we carry a sickle to keep the road we're traveling on clear of weeds and overgrowth. Sometimes the way is quite clear for a while and we wonder if we need to carry such a tool. Conversations are interesting, movies enrich us, anxieties seem far away, and we're wondering whatever happened to temptation in our lives.

Other times the path is hidden by wild growth and we stand, pull, chop, and sweat until we can walk again. Gossip, sexual innuendos, shopping cravings for stuff we don't need or can't afford constantly bite at our heels. Only confronting sin, pulling it out of our lives with repentance and moving on allows us to be called blameless. "The righteousness of the blameless makes a straight way for them" (Prov. 11:5).

The apostle Peter encourages us to make every effort to be found spotless, blameless and at peace with Him (2 Pet. 3:14). Like everything else, God gives us the grace for that effort.

The Guarded Heart

Self-help tests and my husband, Tom, tell me that I am a concrete thinker. I tend to take things literally. Remember Amelia Bedelia of the children's books? That's me. Concrete thinkers need everything spelled out in complete detail or else we miss the main idea because it wasn't mentioned. *What do you mean I was supposed to "dry clean only?" It didn't say that on the label of that silk shawl?*

One scripture very clearly provides a key for living the blameless life for Amelia and me. It is my barometer for any situation: "Above all else guard your heart for it is the wellspring of life" (Prov. 4:23). I pray this for myself every day, and wanting to be like Peter who said as Jesus was washing his feet, "Not just my feet but my hands and my head as well," I also beg, "Not just my heart but my eyes and ears and mouth as well!" (John 13:9)

How do you guard your eyes? I know that there are some things that I can't read if I want to keep a guarded heart. Details of abuse, sexual exploits, or torture do not sit still in my mind, but they agitate me and keep me awake at night, so I cannot let them in. Paying attention to guidelines about book and movie content serves me well. At the video rental store, I check the back of the DVD cover to find out why the rating was given or take advantage of web sites, such as www.Screenit.com, which fill me in on all the detail I might decide to miss.

For many years I didn't read fiction for fear of what I might run into. Interesting characters, a slight flirtation, a late night by the fire and all of a sudden way too many lurid details bombard me! Now I'm wary of certain authors but am carefully enjoying fiction once again. What might be OK for some might not be OK for you or me. Trust God's gut-level leading. You will know when you have not been guarded because the Holy Spirit whispers to your heart. Once again the Psalms speak to me about this. "Turn my eyes away from worthless things" (Ps. 119:37).

Guarding your ears may include walking away from conversations or changing the tone if gossip, husband-bashing, or ethnic slurs are the main menu. Certain songs may lead you down a less than blameless road. TV talk shows might be your point of struggle. Keep your spiritual earplugs handy.

My son played football in high school and was outfitted for the game in massive shoulder pads, hip pads, thigh pads, seat pads, kneepads, spiked shoes, impenetrable helmet and, when he was ready to go out on the field to face the opponent, he slipped a mouth-guard in to protect his teeth. I also need a mouth-guard to remind me not to make an offending comment, exaggerate, or generally grouse. I really wasn't late because "traffic was bad," more accurately, I didn't leave home on time because I was finishing a TV show. "Set a guard over my mouth, O Lord; keep watch over the door of my lips" (Ps. 141:3).

Actively guarding my heart gives me a better chance of being blameless. Recognizing where I haven't been guarded or blameless leads me to repentance, which restores freedom. It is a cycle of spiritual life. Will we ever be sinless? No. The Scripture says, "If we claim to be without sin, we deceive ourselves and the truth is not in us" (1 John 1:8). But we can become quite good at dealing with it quickly.

Jesus has promised to forgive our sins, cover our sins, forget our sins, wipe them out, wash them away, cancel them, and free us. That's His job. Our role is to confess, repent, give them up, hand them over, and get free.

What if you feel trapped? You confess, but it comes right back? Your prayer journal reveals entries about the same sin cycle for many years? Don't quit! God is faithful in His own time. Continue guarding your heart and asking God to reveal any vulnerable points you might have missed. Enlist a trusted friend to pray for you and hold you accountable. Fast for victory and then "After you have done everything . . . stand firm" (Eph. 6:13-14).

Repentance is not a magic formula, but it is the only way to know the full measure of renewal God has for us. Before you move on to restoration, take some time with God to review this chapter. Ask Him to show you how to apply repentance to your life.

Response

How blameless is my life right now?

Where do I need vigilance in guarding my heart?

Where is my trouble spot? My eyes? Ears? Mouth?

When was the last time I had a heart-to-heart conversation with God and genuinely repented of my sins?

The Small Group Speaks

Eloise: Repentance starts with an uneasiness in my spirit and that leads me to seeking the Lord to determine what's going on. If the uneasiness does not happen, I still ask the Lord to show me my heart during my quiet times and this leads to repentance.

Kristy: God usually gets my attention with a sense of conviction, a guilt I can't avoid dwelling on, of which I am so grateful. Also, God uses other means to get my attention like teachings, comments, and life struggles related to the area of sin.

Tara: Usually it comes at the end of a season of struggle. If I have been resisting something or having trouble accepting something from God, I finally reach a point of acceptance. It usually feels like a relief.

Sandy: As usual, God often speaks to me through what I happen to be reading. A theme will develop, and I will see it everywhere.

Rituals of Renewal

- ⚜ Write a prayer telling God you want to be blameless.
- ⚜ Ask a friend to pray for you about your trouble spots.
- ⚜ Ask God to increase your alarm system for guarding your heart.
- ⚜ Look for a time when you won't be rushed and ask God to clean out everything that triggers sin in you.
- ⚜ As a form of confession, write down your sins on pieces of paper and as you repent for each, tear up the paper, shred it, or throw it into the water.

Restoration ... doesn't that happen to furniture? I've seen pieces of "restored" furniture and the before and after pictures don't even look like the same item. Restoration ... I think I'd like some of that for my hair. All the bounce has rubbed off on the inside of my hat and the new shampoo didn't deliver what it promised. Restoration ... I think that happened to the temple in the Bible. There was something about it getting a makeover. Restoration ... You mean ME?

Chapter Three

Restoration

Those stools at the cosmetic counter are enticing. A salesperson dressed like a med student in a white lab coat quickly analyzes your complexion, reaches for little bottles, and starts applying new (usually expensive) products to your face. One especially nice time on a stool resulted in a new color of foundation designed on the spot to exactly match my skin tones (or so they said). Somehow, I never exactly got the same results at my bathroom mirror!

Restoration . . . for my make-up, for my kitchen, for my heart . . . it's usually on my top ten list of daily needs. Is it on God's to-do list for me as well? Sure looks like it from reading His Word.

For years I didn't pay much attention to the 23rd Psalm. It wasn't *my* Psalm; it was *theirs*. It belonged to greeting cards, plaques, and religious people.

I wasn't planning on walking through the valley of the shadow of death any time soon. It was definitely a Psalm for the older generation. I was too busy ruminating over Psalm 51, begging God to have mercy, again! Little did I know that both of these Psalms are about restoration. One morning during a time of desperate dryness, I belatedly took another look at Psalm 23. Wow, why didn't I see this before?

The Personal Shepherd

"The Lord is *my* shepherd . . . " What a possessive statement. He is not just David's shepherd, the "good" shepherd, or the shepherd of Israel. He is *my* shepherd.

I really like that; a personal Shepherd—someone to lead me because He knows where He is going even when I don't. This is better than a life coach! Isn't it such a relief to know that He is right there with us, showing us where the path is each day?

My Shepherd is also in the restoration business. That's kind of an interesting line of work for a shepherd. He clearly states it on his business card, "Restores Souls," and it's right there in the Book. What does that have to do with shepherding? Some of the sheep are quite scraggly, like a cradle I have.

My grandparents and the generations before them farmed in rural Illinois. Five hundred acres of field, one weathered barn, an assortment of sheds, and a tall windmill filled out the landscape. I spent many weekends on that farm as I was growing up. It was quite a contrast to my current urban lifestyle. I liked the two ponds, was afraid of the chickens, and was fascinated by the old house—not the old one my grandparents lived in but the older original house that commonly was referred to as "the old house."

A baby cradle rested in the rafters of the old house. I'm not sure how many generations of "greats" were rocked in that cradle, but family legend would say a lot. When my grandparents died, each grandchild selected one item from the estate before it all went up for grabs. As the oldest, I chose first. I was six months pregnant with my first child and took the cradle.

The paint that covered the natural wood was peeling or gone, bugs of various species had taken up residence in the corners, the rocking coil was hardened with rust. My brothers and cousins were intrigued as to why I would pass on the "good stuff" for something that looked like that! I was confident of its possibilities and dropped it off at a local refinishing business. I don't know what went on in there, but when we picked it up, the cradle was now beautiful, fully restored. In fact, probably better looking than any of the "greats" ever saw it.

All four of our children were lulled to sleep by its gentle motions. Between our babies it was on constant loan to other families who also enjoyed its beauty and its soothing rocking. The cradle is now in the garage collecting cobwebs and waiting for grandchildren. Another fix-up will be needed before it's ready to rock the next generation. Restoration is not a one-time deal.

Restoration isn't just for faces or furniture, my soul needs to be restored at least ten times every day. My "before" picture may show spots chipped away by worry, dry patches from of lack of prayer, cracks from over-scheduling, and bent and broken spots at the joints, just like that old cradle.

How do I get this way? Just like the cradle, wear and tear doesn't happen over night. Sin can cause damage, so does simple neglect, not paying attention to the high need for regular maintenance that we all require. Have you ever had a huge car repair bill just because you forgot to change the oil?

"Restore me . . ." I whisper to the shepherd and the "after" picture begins to emerge like a Polaroid picture; sometimes even immediately. Like a spiritual massage, the calm returns, perspective is renewed; priorities are righted, at least for that moment. Other times, the process isn't as quick but as it gets underway, some degree of relief is usually apparent in response to my pleas.

Restoration is always God's plan A for us. It is a constant theme in Scripture. Restoration is so important to God that He instructed His people to set aside a whole year to it every fifty years, the Year of Jubilee. During this year, all property was returned to the original owners, debts were cancelled, servants were released from duties, and no work was to be done.

God's promise to you and me is the same promise He gave to the Israelites in Joel 2:25: "I will restore the years the locusts have eaten." Each one of us can point to years, months, or days that have been chewed up. Lost opportunities, failed ventures, gulfs in relationships, hardened hearts have left their marks on the landscape of our life's journey. Whatever our circumstances, God's restoration is not only for the day to day, but also for the long run. Take confidence in "The God of all grace…*will himself restore you* and make you strong, firm and steadfast" (1 Peter 5:10, emphasis added).

How does the Lord do His work of restoration? Psalm 23 speaks of two additional pictures of restoration: green pastures and quiet waters. Before you utter your disclaimers about being an urban girl, take a look.

Green Pastures

Even though you may live, as I do, hours away from anything resembling green pastures, the principle is still the same. Just like the green pastures of David's time, I believe this picture represents actual settings God has prepared for us, not just imaginary ideas but real places of refuge, venues of restoration, destinations to fill our spirits back up again.

The Psalm writer doesn't say, "He blesses me when I decide to lay down in green pastures", but rather, "He *makes* me lie down in green pastures." Left on our own, we probably wouldn't even notice the pastures, much less slow down and rest there.

Have you ever driven through beautiful scenery on the interstate so mindlessly that you barely noticed the beauty surrounding you? Driving through Colorado can be like that. At first, you wake up everyone in the car to notice every peak, after awhile, a spectacular summit becomes just one more mountain. Try pulling the car over and walking to the scenic overlook; it is a much different view.

Ever thrown snowballs across the Continental Divide? Did you feel more a part of the mountain experience? How about climbing down a short path to one of those streams on the side of the road, taking off your shoes and testing the water with your toes? Feeling the water is a different sensation than seeing it from the road. This is how God wants to restore us, not just passing through restoration but immersing in it.

Sometimes green pastures look like cafes! For years I had a favorite out-of-the-way French restaurant that served tea and all-you-can-eat bread and jam for a pittance. Beautiful china and soft classical music added to the ambiance. Every Thursday morning, as a matter of habit and obedience, I spread out my books and papers and connected with my lists and myself over cups of tea. I always walked out of there ready to face the world again. Perhaps it was just a place to eat for some, but to me that café was a "green pasture" to restore me.

God chose a garden as the setting for all of creation. Do you have a special garden that restores you? It doesn't have to be in your yard! Beautiful public gardens are accessible in most cities. One of my favorite places to visit is the *Shakespeare Garden* on the campus of Northwestern University in Evanston, Illinois. When life feels like it is closing in, I head there to be restored. Benches line the perimeter of this lovely glade and I have sorted out many life issues by just sitting still while contemplating the gorgeous colors.

A weekend visit to a bed and breakfast is certain to restore, but it doesn't always easily fit into schedule or budget! Consider taking the elements of an inn that are the most soothing to your spirit and bringing them into your home. Quiet music, bright flowers, fun magazines, afternoon tea, and fresh fruit can be yours with minimal cost or effort to create an atmosphere that restores.

Is there an unused area in your home that you could transform into a sanctuary for restoration? Can you create a special place in a corner of your bedroom with a comfortable chair, candle, and pretty basket for your books and magazines? How about a portion of your basement? It is amazing what you can do with an old coal bin!

As the mother of four, living in a small home with one bathroom, finding solitude was a challenge. We live in a former two flat and for many years rented the upstairs apartment. Although we did not share the basement, our tenants stored their seasonal items in a small room downstairs that had formerly been a coal bin. One spring, as the tenants were changing and I was in desperate need of a place of my own, I realized they could store their stuff in the garage and I could have the coal bin! Six hours later, the shelves were out and my chair and books were in. Later that weekend, we painted the walls and hung pictures and put down a garage sale carpet. Adding a CD player for my favorite music and special mementos sprinkled about, I had a place of my own to retreat to whenever I needed to be restored.

Quiet Waters

"He leads me beside quiet waters" is the second method of restoration mentioned in Psalm 23. Scripture is loaded with water analogies. Jesus made several references to living water. This picture from Psalm 23 is repeated in Revelations: "He will lead them to springs of living water" (7:17). Since He is the creator of living water, you can trust that He knows how to find it. Have you ever been at the water's edge with Him? How long has it been? The very last chapter of the Bible, Revelation 22, describes the river of the water of life. Let it bubble at your toes and splash in your face. Let the quiet waters restore you.

My fantasy life always involves an ocean outside the back door or at least down the path. I don't even like to swim, but the ocean triggers all my senses as I hear the waves, see the vast beauty, smell and taste the salt and touch the water with my toes. My first memory of visiting the Atlantic was when I was four years old and it has enchanted me ever since. I now live a twenty-minute walk away from Lake Michigan and stop by as often as I can.

Can you remember being restored by water? Was it a beach on the ocean? A small lake you visited on vacation? A bubbling brook you once hiked by? I recently read about a family who recorded the sound of the bathtub filling with water and played it to lull their baby to sleep.

Does warm water call your name in the form of a long soak with fragrant oils and soft music? Bath pillows are sold for that very reason and a bathroom candle can transform the atmosphere.

Perhaps your quiet waters are not beside a literal lake or river but in another place of stillness that restores you in a similar way. A wooded path? A bicycle trail? An afternoon at home *alone* with a good book or a soft bed and cozy quilt? A cup of cappuccino at a bookstore? Sometimes quiet waters are not a physical place at all, God's restoring transformation inside of us can come in almost any setting.

Restoration comes in the midst of our circumstances, regardless of our season of life. It is not the vacation at the end of the project but the breath of life that flows through it. It is available to us at all times and in all places. The Lord delights to restore us so that we can walk in the truth of his words:

> Those who hope in the Lord will renew their strength. They will soar on wings like eagles. They will run and not grow weary, they will walk and not be faint.
>
> —Isaiah 40:31

Response

How do you know when you need to be restored?

What are your warning signs?
How has the Lord restored you in the past?
Can you name your green pastures and quiet waters?
Describe a restoring atmosphere.

The Small Group Speaks

Kristy: Restoration in my life can be a sister or friend who calls or comes along just at the right time, time alone for some good reading and writing (and a nice salad and glass of iced tea), good music that I enjoy while working, singing, and time alone or with others to pray and encourage each other.

Tara: Since I am nursing a baby through the night and caring for a preschooler who does not nap anymore, I really struggle to find time for restoration. I am learning that I have a fairly strong need for solitude. Not long periods, but I really need some short stretches during each week when I am awake and alone. The beginning of preschool classes a few mornings each week has helped opened up new windows for solitude (if the baby naps during this time!) Solitude is really my favorite form of restoration right now! Having a few books on hand to read when the opportunity arises is wonderful. Just fifteen minutes a day of reading something for pleasure goes a long way for me. Sleep is also very restorative, I am dreaming of the day when it will come in longer stretches, but I take the extra hour or even twenty minutes when the opportunity is there and that can really help restore me as well. Eating really great food, taking a walk, and date nights are also wonderful ways to help me recharge.

Linda: My restoration comes on Saturday mornings when the alarm clock is turned off and there is no reason for me to scurry about and run out the door. My bedroom becomes a place of retreat and renewal. I've found that creating the right setting is very helpful and making my bed and tidying up the room helps to eliminate distractions.

Another place where I meet with God for renewal and refreshing is the forest. This is where God speaks to me like no other. I love to be in natural beauty—and I know that God is waiting for me to step into it. For me it is similar to Dorothy in the *Wizard of Oz* where her everyday surroundings are shades of gray, but when she opens the door of her house after the tornado, she steps into a world alive with color and beauty. It's the same with me in a natural setting; God instantly captures my heart and I feel more alive and one with Him than anywhere else in the world. The only difficulty is getting myself to that place. Because I live in an urban setting, it takes more time and planning. But I know what awaits me, and my heart yearns for it. Everything I see reminds me of God and His creativity and love for this world and for me. It is a safe place.

Not much has to be done to get my heart ready to be in God's presence. With only God's original creation around me, there are no distractions, only hundreds of messages and images of God's love swirling, buzzing, chirping, and swishing all around me and through me. As I drink it all in, I drink in God, His truth, love, beauty, and a deep hunger for more of Him. My heart is opened wide to confess sins, list desires and longings, sing worship songs, and quietly listen to Him speak to me. After spending time like that with Him, it feels better than a month of daily fragrant hot baths, better than a weekend retreat with closest friends, and more rejuvenating than a swim in a pool on a hot summer day. I feel refreshed and more myself and how God created me to be than at any other time. During the time of going through my divorce and the years after, this setting brought deep healing into my crushed heart. It was there among the trees and birds that He taught me to pray and love Him. In the forest I was deeply edified and encouraged to keep going, to keep loving and serving others, and there he taught me how to live out His word and totally depend on Him.

Rituals of Renewal

- Take out a calendar and plan for times of restoration.
- Write a prayer asking for restoration.
- Choose an area for your personal space.
- Begin collecting ideas and props to restore yourself.
- Take a walk by the nearest body of water.
- Visit a beautiful garden in your area.
- Go back to a place that has restored you in the past.
- Browse your favorite books to remind you of how they stirred your soul.
- Visit an art museum.
- Write a letter to an old friend.
- Look through photos from a fun vacation.
- Have lunch at a charming, quaint restaurant.

Reflection . . . caught mine in a store window the other day, oops . . . hem's coming loose on the coat and what's with that slouch? Reflection . . . the way the sun dances on water and shimmers across the surface of the lake in the early morning. Reflection . . . by definition, consideration of some subject matter, idea, or purpose . . . Reflection . . . I think I'll reflect on that as I fall asleep tonight!

Chapter Four

Reflection

Quiet shouts for attention in my life when the blare of the TV, music system, dishwasher, washing machine, vacuum cleaner, e-mail alerts, and even family conversations drown the gentle whisper of the Lord to my spirit. As the volume goes up, my thoughts seem dull, my prayers edge into the vain repetition category, and my dreams fade.

If only there were an extra day every so often or even an additional hour to slow down—yet the calendar is relentless with its pre-filled little boxes. The "free" time that looked so possible a month ago is now sandwiched between two meetings and a lunch date. How can I sort my life out if I can't find it?

Reflection, as a rhythm of renewal, observes the flow of life; it is a time of clearing, considering, and evaluating; it renews and restores. Reflection might lead to planning or decisions but it doesn't start there.

First, it helps to take a good look at "where I've been, where I am, and where I'm going," a practice that is very effective in clearing out the logjams of life. How often we take time to reflect is personal choice, somewhat determined by our season of life as well as our personality. The pace, style, tools, and settings of reflection vary. Ask God to show you which of the many available options will fit you best, at least for now.

Pace of Reflection

Random reflection flows through our days. Drive-time, wait-time, shower-time all provide the mindless backdrop for stray thoughts to dance across our mental screens. Some would call it daydreaming. An issue or an event pops up and we choose to ponder it, take it apart a bit, and view it from a few different angles. Often our time runs out, we arrive at our destination, our name gets called, the hot water runs out, the shade to our window of reflection is yanked down; we're back to the details of life.

Random reflection has its place and occasionally a stray shower thought becomes the building block for our next season of life. Women in search of renewal, however, make time for intentional reflection. How much time? We decide at our pace based on our own felt needs.

Daily reflection in times of quiet is essential for some of us. Rewinding the day, reviewing goals, and planning for the days ahead is vital to us. Usually, early morning or right before bed-time are favorite slots to review and plan. How did I spend my time, my money? Did I make progress with my goals? Do I need to make any amends? What am I grateful for today? List makers don't call it a day till they get their items crossed off or transferred to another day.

Weekly reflection helps shape the days ahead. Taking a look at the week ahead for scheduling, meal planning, and family coordination helps to live an intentional life. Weekly reflection can also provide opportunity to decide when to see a friend, take a longer walk, or browse a bookstore—the essentials of life that don't come with a pre-fixed time. Sunday afternoon or evening is often an ideal time to take stock of the week ahead.

Anne Ortlund, author of *Disciplines of the Beautiful Woman* takes a day each month for planning and evaluating her goals.

Twelve days or three percent of the year seems like a modest investment to stay on track. A half-day, or even a few hours each month, will let you know where you're in the grand scheme of things and bring you the benefits of order. For quite awhile I set aside one Saturday morning a month to stay in my pajamas, listen to quiet music and plan goals for the next month. The plan worked well till my season of life changed again!

Seasonal or quarterly reflection based upon the calendar, the weather, or school schedules establishes a pace of reflecting that is easy to remember. Most of us know our seasonal rhythms and know how to project for one calendar segment based on our style of moving through the year. I seem to have much more productive energy in the spring and fall, more inner flow in the winter, and love to be out and about in the summer, so I adapt my life planning according to that cycle.

There are many devotees of annual reflection. For some women, a quick scramble to throw together a to-do list for the next year seems to work while others prefer an extensive evaluation of all the areas of their lives. Over the January weekend closest to New Year's Day, I love to reread my journal from the past year to remember all that touched my life and shaped me. The pages then get filed away and the new book begins. I have also found that I plan better when I'm done with the holiday season, which sometimes isn't till mid-January.

For some of us, our real New Year starts in the fall. It is amazing the huge mental shift that can occur when the calendar page turns from August to September! Annual reflection as the beach towels get put away and the sweaters come out can shape life direction for the next twelve months.

Birthdays are another regular reminder that a year has passed! A birthday ritual of taking stock of the past year and looking ahead to the next can be a looked-forward-to component of the celebration. For a woman who is somewhat settled in her season of life, a single longer annual reflection to fine-tune her life can be sufficient. Others may need to take stock more frequently.

Styles of Reflection

There are many different ways to structure life reflection and they all work! Goal settings, priority defining, an ongoing to-do list, and categories of life are all effective styles of reflection.

It has been said that "goals are dreams with deadlines." Reflective women who set goals to realize their dreams structure their lives along those lines. Where do I want to be in five years? One year? Next month? End of this week? Today? Diligent goal-setters enjoy browsing their life map destinations. How am I doing in my plans to read through the Bible? Am I on track for my self-imposed deadline of finishing my degree? Will our financial goals be met in time for vacation? Goal setters who enjoy reflection see it as an affirming exercise because they usually ARE on track.

Priority ranking is also a way to organize reflection. One method to evaluate priorities is to ask where our time, energy, and money are going. Are they in line with the stated desires of our heart? *If these are my priorities, how are they working out in my life?* If you have never clearly defined your priorities, taking time to do that can be very valuable. Once you have defined your priorities (i.e. family, friends, church, time and money management, healthy eating patterns) it will be easier to see if you are on track.

Another approach to sorting out our lives is the use of categories. One example of this is the framework of "I want to *be*," "I want to *do*," "I want to *have*." All that we want to grow into, accomplish, and obtain can fit into these categories. Keeping a fluid list close at hand of each category will help us stay focused.

One mother I know uses the four qualities ascribed to Jesus in Luke 2:52 to organize her reflections on her children. "And Jesus grew in wisdom and stature, and in favor with God and men." She uses this pattern to look at the intellectual, physical, spiritual, and social development of her children. We may use the same grid to reflect upon our own lives. Using categories like these personalize the reflection process and it's easy to change the content with the circumstances.

These are not meant to imply, "choose all the above," but find *one* style of reflection that seems to fit your personality. You will likely use a number of styles of reflection over all your seasons of life!

Settings for Reflection

Even random reflection requires a setting where the mind can be clear enough to process connected thoughts. Can you imagine what a planned setting can do? Take a moment to remember which settings invite you into a deeper place of thought.

Walking works for many. Even a short stroll around the block can trigger reflection. Sometimes it is the scenery that inspires. A walk by a pond, in the forest, or on a nature trail can transport you to a different place in your thought process. Even walking on familiar sidewalks can open up awareness to a deeper agenda as you take one step after another. Can you look for opportunities to add a short walk to your daily round? Besides the exercise and endorphin benefits, opening up your mind in fresh ways is likely to occur.

Taking yourself out to tea or for a meal alone with your journal and note pad is another way to create a setting for creative reflection. Getting outside of your home deals with many distractions and enjoying food that someone else has prepared is very conducive to relaxation, which can be an invitation to reflect. Can you discover a nearby place to slip into for personal replenishment and creative thinking over a hot drink and a scone?

Water lovers may find their setting in the most private room of the house, the *boudoir* or the bathroom. Candlelight, the fragrance of scented oils, a bath pillow to rest on, could be part of the indulgence. Hang on to all those reflective thoughts though, as writing them down might be a soggy exercise.

This past January, I sat in the large lobby of a nearby retreat center for five hours and planned the next few months. Because I was not using a room or eating meals there (I brought my own lunch) there was no charge. When I needed to stretch, I could take a walk on the grounds. Reflection came easily at a place like that.

Hotel lobbies, especially during the week, are also good places to curl up in a corner area and sort out life. What is available in your area? Find a place that works now, and when you're ready for a new setting, look around, it won't be far away.

Tools of Reflection

An artist needs her paints, brushes, smock, canvas, or sketchpad. Interior designers require paint samples, fabric swatches, graph paper, and room dimensions. Culinary hobbyists can't do without fresh food, spices, mixing bowls, utensils, and an assortment of cooking pots. Planned reflection involves tools of some sort to set the tone, trigger the thoughts, and record the results.

What kinds of tools? Whatever works! Here are some of mine.

Music

Instrumental worship pieces, soaring movie themes, stirring classical arrangements all call forth my creativity and reflective frame of mind. Choosing the music to fit the agenda adds another layer to the reflection ritual and becomes for that moment part of the soundtrack of my life.

Favorite Books

One bookshelf in my writing room holds only my favorite books. They have become my favorites because they have shaped me the most. Just looking at them inspires me to reach higher, and a quick glance at that shelf is all it takes to clear my mind and remind me of John Kieran's quote, "I am a part of all I have read." I'll take one or two along for inspiration on a planned reflective outing.

Lists

Ahhh, the sight of an empty page on a legal pad entices me. Lists can hold goals, priorities, lists of categories, resolutions, and projects. I can get so carried away! Reflection often starts with lists or ends there. Lists can stay on the lined pages or note cards or get neatly transferred to Filofaxes, Day Timers, kitchen calendars, PDAs, or computers. It doesn't matter how you preserve the lists, just find the most practical and useful way to keep a record.

I like a medium-size spiral notebook that fits in my large purse and carries my ongoing to-do list. Whenever anything pops in my mind, from buying batteries to filling out insurance forms, it all goes on the same list. Later I might sort the items out, but the fun is always in crossing off items as they are completed.

Life list...The ultimate list for the whole of one's life. In the course of my lifetime, I want to (fill in the blank). A life list is a measurable tool of things to cross off as they are done. See the Grand Canyon, learn to ride a horse, see Chicago from the top of the Sears Tower, read the whole Bible, master conversational Spanish, ride in a helicopter, and so on. The list is YOURS, so it reflects your passions and interests. I keep mine in my prayer journal and look at it once a week to see if I can make progress or add something else.

Journals

As a tool of reflection, a journal can help sort out life's issues. Stating a perplexing issue and then writing and answering such questions like why is this so important/confusing/hard to me? What do I hope to accomplish? Where do I want to be in a year? A journal can be an incredible tool for ordering your inner agenda.

Writing love letters to God on loose-leaf paper as well as recording the desires of my heart and angst of my soul has been part of my morning ritual for a long time. Usually I have much more to write about on days of joy and days of pain, but there is something recorded nearly everyday. Prayer journals remind me where my heart has been, my cries to my Father, and how I have seen his hand at work in my life.

> *Oh Father, here I am again full of anxiety. Remind me of Your faithfulness. Please shape me into the kind of woman who is not twisted by circumstances but rather refined. Show me Your face in this hard time.*
>
> *You are an amazing God! You know me so well and show up in the most fun ways!*

My prayer journals are for *me* alone. My family knows where they are and will have access to them after my death! Sometimes I write cryptically so my children won't know which one was piercing my heart on any given day, but honesty and transparency in my prayers is what works to really connect me to God.

As the self-appointed family historian, I also keep a daily journal of family life in simple blank books by writing a few lines per day, a simple recounting exercise. Unlike the prayer journals, these are in a prominent place and available to be read at any time. Often they are used as a reference. *What year did Uncle Brad and Aunt Cindy stay with us? Who did I go to that dance with? When did I have chickenpox?* These journals bring back the sweet moments of family life and paint the scenes all over again like re-watching an old favorite movie.

Some women keep an all-purpose journal for recording information, taking notes, sorting ideas, making goals. It is an eclectic written record of one's entire life. You can use a fancy book, notebook, loose-leaf paper, or artist's sketch book. Date it and try to be completely honest. It is for you. You can leave instructions to destroy upon your demise if that makes you feel better!

Personal Retreats

Many of us have been on women's retreats. Good teaching, lots of voices joined in worship, optional workshops, mediocre food, and usually a fair night's sleep. Retreats play a role in our growth in the Lord, and I highly recommend them as a place to build relationships, gain inspiration, and just get away for a night or two.

A personal retreat is just for you and the Lord. It provides concentrated time for personal reflection. My first ten years of semi-annual private retreats took place at a convent near my home that had developed a section of the building for private retreats. Meals and use of the beautiful grounds were included in the modest fee. Occasionally, if I really needed to stay close to home, I would borrow a friend's home for the day while she was out. I was away from MY laundry, MY floors to clean, MY dishes to wash. Even if I was in someone else's home, I had none of the daily responsibility.

I discovered a charming bed and breakfast that's about an hour's train ride from my home. You can do a lot with twenty-four hours, but I encourage women to take longer if time and money allow. Consider using a personal day from work or comp time for your get-away time. The first few hours can be spent unwinding by light reading, a walk, bath, or nap. When I finally feel detached from all that's undone at home I pray for God's wisdom and direction and start responding in prayer and writing down ideas. Taking stock of current areas of my life and reflecting about where I've been and where I'm going comprise most of the retreat time.

Bringing my reflections to the Lord piece by piece as they unfold and asking His guidance and blessing are essential components. Music in the background and a cup of tea at my side are a part of the atmosphere as well.

As a rhythm of renewal, reflection is essential. The pace, style, tools, and setting can vary but the results will be consistent. Discover your personal flavor of this life-giving practice.

Response

Does your reflection time most often come in random or planned form?

What tools would you need for a good reflection time?

Describe the pace and style that would work for you.

When can you schedule a personal retreat?

The Small Group Speaks

Glenna: I have a mix of tools for reflection plus the input of my closest friends to help me along the path God's laying out. One tool is a general journal, which I don't feel compelled to write in it every day. I write intercessory prayers for myself and others; I tell God things I'm thinking about; I copy portions of Scripture that have been particularly meaningful to me, perhaps including why; and I also sometimes include brief passages of the writings of others that are particularly meaningful to me. My journal is an intimate connecting place with Christ.

Another favorite tool, one I more recently picked up, is the habit of reading *The Daily Light* every day. It is a compilation of Scriptures—a set for the morning and one for the evening and more meditative. Another major tool for reflection is whatever Bible study I'm doing at the time, whether it's a Beth Moore study, a Kay Arthur Precepts study, or a Dee Brestin study.

I also regularly download teachings by people who I believe offer a unique and fresh perspective on faith issues and I listen while walking or jogging, which makes for a wonderful time of reflection on a beautiful day outdoors, as I'm also soaking in the beauty of my neighborhood or maybe some more majestic location if we're on a trip.

Even though I still experience impatience with what seems like God's slowness in pointing me in the right direction, I've changed my expectations and understanding over the years regarding how God works in my life. I am more likely to trust that God is in fact hearing my prayers and responding, even if I don't see immediate evidence. I've become more willing and able to wait for the Lord, and I see all of my reflective process as an act of waiting. In addition, I've felt the Lord prompting me towards more of a "just for this day" practice along the lines of "give us this day our daily bread."

Tara: My reflection times are different now with two young children. I have signed up for a year long Bible study program with weekly study questions. I usually break up this assignment—about ninety minutes—into shorter fifteen- or thirty-minute stretches during the week. It is not every day, more often three days a week. Sometimes it is on the couch of the lobby where I sit with my napping baby while Christian is in preschool. Sometimes it is in bed after the kids are asleep. Sometimes it is during an uncommon lull in the afternoon while Christian is self-occupied. I am enjoying the structure of this program for now. When I have my assignment done for the week, I am done. And I do not have any sense of guilt or obligation that I should be doing something more or something every day.

Deb: Currently my best reflection—and prayer time— is while walking in the early mornings along our country road. The dogs accompany me, delighted in my company without requiring any attention, and they don't mind my verbal musings, though the occasional passer-by might wonder who I am talking to! Sometimes just stepping out the door can help change perspective.

Sandy: Each year since I became a Christian, I've made spiritual goals, some years more elaborate than others. This year, I decided to take a break. I still made out my goals, but I tried to keep them as simple as possible, so as to have a year of rest. However, one new tool has emerged this year: an illustrated commonplace book. Each time God reveals a truth to me, I've made a page in the book, using collage techniques. Looking for the images to represent God's lessons has slowed me down in a new way, really helping me to work through the teaching. It's also been a great way to look back over the recent past when I've been faced with a new challenge.

Rituals of Renewal

- Browse a stationary store for fun pens and calendars.
- Define what kind of music sets the stage for your reflection.
- Set aside a few hours in the next month for planning.
- Buy a large dry erase calendar for long-range planning.
- Decide your personal pace for reflection.
- Sort out your favorite books.
- Start creating a life list.
- Shop for a journal that will be fun to use.
- Create a reflection ritual that will work for you.

Rituals . . . the church I grew up in had a lot of them. The really religious people seemed to know what to do with them. Rituals . . . Is that the opposite of random? Rituals . . . "A system or form of rites, religious or otherwise" (Webster). *I wonder what the "otherwise" ones are? Rituals . . . I hope they're not just one more thing to do.*

Chapter Five

Rituals

Six P.M. on any given Saturday is pizza night at our house. It begins as I wander into the kitchen and begin flipping through my collection of CDs. Crooning along to a Frank Sinatra album, I pre-heat the oven, take out the food processor, and set it on the counter and place the simple dough into it. While the dough is rising, I quickly assess what ingredients I have and what delectable leftovers would make a great pizza. Leftover chicken usually means Mexican-style pizza. Spinach, garlic, and feta cheese often become an aromatic veggie pizza. Forty-plus minutes later the aroma draws the family into the kitchen, and we sit down to dinner.

Rituals anchor my day and enhance the ordinary tasks of life. The order in which things are done, the attention paid to the details of an activity, the carefully chosen props for each task at hand, all create a ceremony of sorts that provides meaning and significance to the ordinary events of the day.

Personal rituals shape who we are by calling us back to our essential selves. My rituals are my "stamp of identity" and when I get off balance, returning to them grounds me once again. In my ongoing quest for renewal, returning to or creating rituals is one of the foundational steps.

Most of us already participate in rituals of all sorts, though we may have never called them that. Making the coffee, reading the paper, or checking the stock market are all common activities in the early part of the day. How does one define a set of tasks as a "ritual"? Certain elements are present that set them apart from the long to-do lists that occupy our days.

Elements of a Ritual

Intentionality

Participating in a ritual is a choice; it does not "just happen." Intentionality, "I'm choosing to do this (task, activity) in this same way again and again," sets rituals apart from other activities. Most rituals are repeated, often daily.

Athletes, writers, dancers, and artists often follow prescribed patterns when entering into the task at hand. Rituals will help just as well. Begin with setting aside time to focus before beginning any task and consciously pay attention to the details. Sometimes actually saying aloud, "Now I am going to start my morning/bedtime/bill paying ritual" will help you focus on what is about to happen. A certain reverence accompanies each task when a choice has been consciously made to participate once again.

One chosen ritual is the common practice of blessing food before eating. Our intentionality often starts with a decision to *always* give thanks for food. There's no need to ask yourself each time, "Should I bless the food?" because the choice is already made regardless of where you are. The blessing may be silent, spoken, or sung; from a scripted prayer or spontaneous, holding hands or bowing heads, but the ritual of giving thanks before eating will take place.

Order

A ritual has a clear beginning and end. You are aware of when it has started and when it is over. The order of a ritual can be determined by a variety of factors.

Clock time

A morning ritual may begin when you get up and end forty minutes later. Other rituals that are clock determined can include bedtime or mealtime patterns. When I was a child, my Dad worked ten minutes away from home and always left the office promptly at 5 P.M. At 5:05 every night, my mom would set the table and put empty pots on the stove so "it would look like dinner was started!" We laugh about it now, but it was a very endearing ritual to welcome my dad home!

Events

Daily events, as well as once in a lifetime events, often follow a scripted pattern. When your children come home from school, the ritual begins when you sit with them for a snack and talk about their day and it ends when they go start their homework or head off to play. A wedding begins when the mothers are escorted to their seats and ends when the bride and groom walk down the aisle. Think about events in your life and see if you can find the ritual thread. If your personality tends to be random, find some time and prayer to consider where rituals would bring helpful order to your day and increase efficiency and where they would restrict you.

Tasks

Ordinary household or work duties can also evolve into rituals by observing where they begin and end. A gardening ritual could start with mindfully putting on a sunhat, gathering the tools, and blessing the soil; and it could end when the hose is rolled up and the hat comes off. A bill paying ritual can be created by first putting on soothing music, then carefully setting out the bills, calculator, checkbook, and stamps or opening up the computer financial program. It ends when the bills are placed in the mailbox or scheduled to be paid.

Spring cleaning is a task that can be enjoyable, comforting, and renewing by elevating it to a ritual. It can start with circling the date on the calendar and shopping for new cleaning supplies and end with a sparkling home and a special spring cleaning meal!

Seasonal Calendars

The rhythm of the seasons provides a natural order to many rituals. Planting in the spring and harvesting in the fall has been a ritual in many parts of the world since the beginning of time. Putting away hats and mittens and getting them out again can be seen as a ritual if mindfulness is added to it. Celebrating the first snow with hot cocoa or the first day of spring with a picnic are all rituals that flow with the order of the seasons.

Liturgical Calendars

Many church based rituals follow the order of liturgical rhythms and calendars. The tolling of the Catholic church's Angelous bell marked time for noon prayers; lighting a new candle each week in the Advent wreath lets us know Christmas is getting closer. Ashes on the forehead announce the beginning of Lent; the silencing of the bells marks Good Friday. I enjoy observing my Jewish friends making room in their schedules for the rituals that correspond to the holidays of their faith. The housecleaning for Passover, building huts for Sukkot, planning carnivals for Purim are all examples of rituals determined by faith traditions.

Props

Many rituals include objects of some sort to help enhance the experience. Here are just a few examples.

Candles

Candles are lit at the beginning of a ritual and blown out at the end. The Jewish Sabbath meal on Friday nights begins with this ritual. Many dinners, personal ceremonies, and conversations start this way. I like to light a candle during the winter months before my morning prayer time.

Readings

Starting a ritual with a devotional reading, a familiar quote or poem, or a prayer and ending with the same puts figurative parentheses around the event.

Clothing

Sometimes clothing is a key ingredient in a ritual. Changing into something comfortable after work, putting on stretchy clothes before a morning exercise routine, donning a fun apron to start preparing food are all examples.

Food/drink

Sharing a toast, breaking the bread, and pouring the tea are all components of certain rituals. Think of the role of a cake in a birthday or wedding celebration, oyster soup on Christmas Eve, ham on Easter. When food is scripted, there is usually a ritual involved!

Music

Many rituals include a background score. Bills can be paid to classical music, dining enhanced by jazz in the background, creative writing encouraged to flow with movie soundtracks, and praying more focused with Gregorian chants. Officially starting the holiday season by playing the first Christmas CD, Handel's *Messiah*, is a ritual I look forward to each year.

Enjoyment

Rituals can enhance our lives in such a way that we look forward to engaging in them. Many mornings the thought of the toast, tea, and quiet time propels me out of bed. When we design our own rituals, we are invested in the details and a sense of ownership adds to the experience.

On Monday nights, during my youngest daughter's middle school years, we would often share a tea party. This was a great way to connect with her. We prepared a tea tray with special cookies that we ate only at this time and brought it to my bed.

Bach would play in the background and we would rewind the events of the day. Sometimes the tea party only lasted about twenty minutes, but it was a ritual worth keeping.

The family might participate in certain holiday traditions, but a few personal rituals accompany these celebrations and give me great enjoyment. My own holiday rituals include an annual reading of the Christmas Carol sometime each December, reviewing my journal on New Year's Eve, picking out a Valentine to send to my husband's office, and changing the day-to-day dishes from a winter pattern to a summer one on Memorial Day.

I also have a few anniversaries of the heart that only I celebrate! Every May 11 is First Communion Day to remember one of my favorite childhood days. February 16 is a time for celebration that began when I was about nine and realized on this day that spring was coming soon. June 12 started out as an ordinary day in 1990 but was full of all my favorite elements of a quintessential summer, so it always gets celebrated as well.

One ritual that illustrates all these components is a personal bedtime ritual. Establishing a bedtime ritual for ourselves, just as we once did for our own young children, can help us sleep well. It starts with the *intention* of heading to bed before exhaustion has settled in. The *order* becomes visible if you start the ritual by turning off the lights in parts of the house and saying goodnight to anyone around. The *props* might include carefully chosen products for cleansing and creaming, comfortable pajamas, good light for reading, and a favorite bedtime book. Complete this bedtime ritual by calling to mind your satisfying moments of the day and turn out the light. *Enjoy* this bedtime ritual enough to repeat it each night!

Rituals elevate the ordinariness of life into something special. Intentionally choosing to participate in a life experience in a certain order, using props to enhance the moment, and enjoying the lift that it brings to our lives is not only a ritual for a segment of time but of renewal for all of our life.

Response

Do you remember any rituals you created as a child?

Are you intentional about creating rituals as an adult?

Are you satisfied with the rituals you currently engage in? Do you have a favorite?

What rituals would you like to institute?

The Small Group Speaks

Glenna: Many years ago, I practiced several personal rituals which provided a structure that seemed to make everything work well enough for me to feel secure or safe—although I didn't identify it as filling that need at the time. I just knew that if I didn't run my five miles at a certain time every day, or couldn't follow through on all of my personal bedtime rituals, I felt very unsettled and irritable. My first understanding of how these personal rituals might actually have a negative side was the depression I'd feel when we went on a vacation and my routines and rituals would be interrupted. Whether it was the change in location that might preclude carrying out some of the rituals, or holiday activities that interfered (even fun things I'd looked forward to), I felt like my moorings had come loose, and I'd begin to just want to go home—back to my trusted rituals. A friend suggested that I develop a new ritual to fit a specific holiday trip or location—something that would help me feel a reasonable sense of structure rather than the chaos I was experiencing. So, one of my favorite holiday rituals is to find a novel I'm sure

I will love and read it every chance I get while we're gone—specifically, sitting by a pool or on the beach! This is significant because I do NOT read novels at any other time. Also, I will join my husband in one of his vacation rituals, like morning coffee on the balcony, which is not especially important to me, but joining him creates good memories.

Raising children and coping with my husband's intense travel schedule also made it difficult to keep up my personal rituals, and I had to learn to be flexible about practicing them, as well as to not count on them to provide the main structure in my life or sense of peace. As a result of opening myself to flexibility, I developed a sense of adventure, which really was lacking before; and this came in quite handy when we moved overseas! When we lived in Singapore and then Shanghai, I had developed small rituals and rhythms, mostly out of necessity, which were unique to those locations. For me, setting up helpful rituals came more naturally in an unusual environment than in my home country.

Deb: What began as a need for more exercise has become an essential beginning to the day. As soon as I roll out of bed I pull on my walking clothes and pick up the leash. A brisk two-mile walk along the country road wakes me up and gives me the opportunity to think and to pray as the day begins. The dog does not mind my prayers or my tears. This daily ritual has created a framework for my life and puts prayer in the first thing of each day.

The "Friday Ritual" started when I was living in the city many years ago. I began spending Fridays with another mom and her young children. Together we would take the children to a park and have lunch or, if the weather was not cooperative, spend the afternoon in one of our homes. This became a ritual that has carried us through twenty years. Our lives and schedules have changed as children have been added and then left home; jobs and homes have changed, but spending part of Friday together whenever possible throughout the years has anchored our friendship and kept us steady and sane through the many changes along the road.

I also appreciate seasonal rituals. Summer days are exhausting. Like a bee, I feel compelled to keep working as long as the daylight lasts. Planning lessons for the coming school year, gardening, tackling household projects, and a thousand other tasks fill the days. Winter comes as a much needed season of rest. When the days become short and the wind blows from the north, we put extra quilts on the beds and tuck the house in for the winter. Evenings can be spent playing Scrabble, catching up on photo albums, or snuggled in blankets with favorite movies. Spring will come and with it new growth and busy activity. Trees are not expected to bear fruit all year round, and even evergreens wait until spring to send out new growth. The realization that I do not have to be equally "productive" each day allows me to enjoy each season in its time.

Sandy: Due to my business' schedule, Monday is my Saturday and needs to include time for both rest and chores. I do vary my routine, but at least twice a month, I have a much-looked-forward-to ritual:

"coffee and candles." After I drop off Jack at school, I stop by Starbucks, then return home and pop in one of two CDs, light a scented seasonal candle, and tidy, sort mail, and do laundry. The morning passes, the chores get done and something about the music and the candle totally relaxes me! I feel great! Then I have until school gets out to read, work on a project, take a nap, or whatever!

Rituals of Renewal

- Brainstorm ideas for rituals for each season of the year.
- Start a collection of products for your bath such as a loofah, gels, and bath pillow.
- Try a hot bath before dinner to segue into the evening.
- Purchase candles with a variety of scents to use for personal rituals.
- Review your anniversaries of the heart and decide how to observe them.
- Stock up on specialty teas and cookies and paraphernalia for tea parties. Schedule tea time like the Brits!
- Supply your desk area with pretty pens and cards to write personal notes. Plan a weekly ritual to write one note to an old friend.
- Experiment with starting and ending the day with selections from the *Book of Common Prayer.*
- Find a fun apron to wear for special meal preparations.
- Reread your favorite books from childhood each winter.
- Decide which holiday traditions you want to start.
- Celebrate your birthday each year with a personal ritual to celebrate your life.

Reordering . . . It's time for some change around here! I think that wing chair would look almost new if I moved it against the east wall, instead of by the window. Maybe I'll plant white tulips in front of the hedge this year. It's time to update those old pictures on the piano. My filing system needs help if I'm ever going to find those receipts for taxes. Reordering . . . I think I'll find a new time management book!

Chapter Six

Reordering

As a girl, I loved changing the clocks in the spring to daylight savings time. That was my signal to rearrange my bedroom furniture. My mom and I worked on it together until I was old enough to handle it myself. My bed, dresser, nightstand, bookcase, and vanity were all pulled out into the hall so the floor could be cleaned. That was the boring part.

Windows were cleaned first since, as long as the room was empty, it would save me climbing on the furniture later to get them. This was more rewarding than the floor as I could actually see a before and after difference.

Next came the fun part—bringing back the furniture. Each year I tried to find a new place for the bed. Under the windows? Next to the door? Anywhere it would fit was an option, as long as it was a change from last year. Into the laundry went the heavy bedspread and out of the closet came the lighter weight cotton one. The nightstand had to fit close enough for reading at night by the light of the lamp that perched on top, but its placement could be played with.

I loved to spend time rearranging my books each year. They were lined up by author one year, by category the next, sometimes by size, and one time by color. Those yellow *Nancy Drew* books looked so nice next to the other book jackets. Interspersed with the books were pictures, mementos and my current collection of treasures; seashells one year, bells the next.

Each item had to pass my scrutiny, get wiped off, displayed in a new spot or get relegated to the closet for this season.

The dresser was another big project. Until early summer in the Midwest, it was still possible to need a sweater one day and shorts the next so for a while the drawers were bulging with clothes for all seasons. I enjoyed the sorting out process: setting aside the pieces that I had outgrown or those that had finally gone out of style and the clothes I just never wanted to wear again. I greeted my summer clothes like old friends. My green shorts! My yellow tank top! How nice to see you again!

By the end of the rearranging day, the pillows were plumped in perfect order, books were ready to browse, summer togs waited in drawers and I was sure that *this time* I would keep my room neat all summer. It was a wonderful day.

In the fall, rearranging was easier. Change the bedspread back to the heavy one, tidy up the books, put away the shorts, and bring out the tights. It was a simpler, yet still satisfying, ritual. Because the need for renewal is woven into our spirits, reordering and rearranging is often an expression of that renewal. For most women, our homes are where we focus our attention.

Women—The Heart of the Home

Women have the privilege of being the "heart" of the home. We check the pulse of our husband and children and are aware of the state of the union of our family at any given time. We have our intuitive antennas up so we know when to encourage, say a prayer, or when to back off when needed. We also seem to know where the holes need to be patched in day-to-day life and we try to fill those as we go along.

Being the heart of the home involves shaping the home environment to help the family thrive. Our homes are intended to be a shelter, a haven, and a nurturing base for all who live there, including the mom! Shaping can involve everything—from choosing the color of the cereal dishes to turning on the night-light for bedtime prayers.

Cycles of reordering and rearranging set the stage for creating an atmosphere that warms and enfolds. Reordering your home is an ongoing project. Painters of the Golden Gate Bridge, after finally completing painting the entire bridge, must go back to the beginning and start all over because by then it needs it again.

Our homes are like that. We have a picket fence in our back-yard that needs maintenance every year. Poles rot, the paint chips, the pickets crack. Parts of it need to be regularly rebuilt to survive another summer. Most of us have projects like this.

In our spiritual lives, when God wants to get our attention, He usually focuses on just one area at a time to so we don't get overwhelmed. That's a good tactic for our homes as well because our household to-do list often exceeds our life expectancy!

A good place to start is at the front door. Go outside and walk up your sidewalk. What do you see? Flowers in the yard or a wreath on the door are signposts of welcome. Would you feel welcome to visit here just by the appearance of the outside of your home? Is your address easily readable from the street? We live on a corner so our yard has full visibility from two streets. When our four children were small, so many yard toys were on display that people often assumed we were operating a daycare center. Folks make assumptions by what they see. What part of the outside of your home needs reordering?

Step inside your home. What is the first thing you see? Is there anything you would like to change about it? Move slowly through your home, perhaps taking twenty minutes at a time to observe, make notes, putter around, and decide the next step. It can help to actually set a timer for twenty minutes, try not to leave the room until you've finished with your observation.

My love for rearranging furniture has stayed with me. A new seating arrangement in the living room, switching the sideboard and the piano in the dining room, discovering a new placement for a king size bed in our small bedroom are all points of triumph. More than a hobby, changing things around helps create and shape the home. This home is fresh, resonating life and renewal. We are not stagnant and neither are our homes.

If moving the furniture around is not an option, play with other items in the room. Can you change a lampshade? Recover the couch pillows? Hang the pictures on different walls or even in a different room? I have a collection of small-framed photos of my children at various ages and I love to move them around.

The mementos and objects that we look at every day and occasionally dust around are the artifacts of our culture as a family. Over time our interests may change and what seemed so personally defining ten years ago may have lost its significance. Part of rearranging is replacing. If you can't bear to permanently part with something, box it up and store it in the basement or garage until you're ready let it go.

We can be decorators in our own homes by painting, stenciling, wallpapering, trying different window coverings, and experimenting with rugs. Some of us are born with these talents; others hire them or call friends. All of us can shape the little touches by changing the tablecloth on the dining room table, trying a lace doily under a lamp, restacking books, or adding pictures to a hallway.

Yard and garage sales are a wonderful source for decorative pieces and new supplies at rock bottom prices. I am so inspired to reorder my home after a morning of allowing "garage sale" signs to determine my route. People move, redecorate, clean out, and are eager to get rid of their stuff. Haggling over the price is usually part of the fun, and if your new acquisition turns out not to fit after all, you're not out much.

Most of our kitchens could use some reordering. We become blind-sighted to what we see every day. The top of the fridge can be a landing strip for items we've forgotten we owned. The plants may have died a few weeks back, but we didn't notice. Announcements for events that have already taken place still decorate the sides of our refrigerators. Spices for recipes we no longer make take space in our cabinets. The tastes we identified at the time of our wedding showers have probably been refined since then. Do we recognize our current self in our dishes, place-mats, and candleholders? Often it is time to give our selves a new "shower," one item at a time.

As we survey our rooms, keep in mind the question . . . Is this the atmosphere we want to create for our families or is it one that just happened? In her book, *Hidden Art*, Edith Schaeffer writes, "And for the Christian who is consciously in communion with the Creator, surely his home should reflect something of the artistry, the beauty and order of the One whom he is representing, and in whose image he has been made!" Reordering and rearranging can contribute to revealing something of this artistry.

Nurture Yourself

When I stay overnight at a bed and breakfast inn, I generally feel pampered, special, cared for. As a result of that sense of well-being, I subsequently feel creative, inspired, and somehow encouraged in life. It's not that their breakfast eggs are so much better than mine or that the wallpaper is prettier, although that might be! The major difference seems to lie in the details. At places like these, all the details line up to shape the atmosphere. The choice of colors, fabrics, china, background music, and tea service are part of a collective whole that works to restore.

By paying attention to the details of our surroundings, we create a place that is nurturing for those we love. We use the props around the home to help support. We create the backdrop, the stage as it were, for life to play out; and, in so doing, we influence the outcome of the players. That is part of our role as the heart of the home.

For this we do not need a degree in interior design, a lot of cash or even large chunks of time. Although some renovations can take a long time and rearranging furniture can take hours, most ongoing reordering can be done in short spurts. As the gardener goes through the rows and hedges, trimming here and pulling weeds there, so we too can approach our homes.

Reordering and rearranging nurtures our families and ourselves. These tasks can call forth the inspiration and creativity which all of us possess. To view loving our homes only as "housework" diminishes this role of shaping the atmosphere of the home. Rhythms of renewal touch all points of our lives. As Samuel Johnson said, "To be happy at home is the ultimate result of all ambition, the end to which every enterprise and labor tends."

Response

Do you tend to reorder seasonally or as needed?
Describe the personal results of reordering?
Do you prefer to rearrange alone or with your family's help?
Which area in your home would you like to start with?

The Small Group Speaks

Deb: As a result of frequent moves during my childhood, rearranging furniture when NOT moving has never had much of an appeal to me. The ideal reordering of my surroundings takes place in the kitchen.

Decorative display shelves sit above the buffet in my large country kitchen. During the fall season, these shelves hold my autumn fruit-patterned plates, bowls and platters. Coordinating color mugs fill in the spaces. I add Thanksgiving turkey salt-and-pepper shakers and ceramic Pilgrim figures as the holiday approaches. The fall dishes are packed away before the first Sunday in Advent when the Christmas china makes its appearance and sets the kitchen in a holiday mood. We use the Christmas china most days during Advent. It makes even a humble bowl of soup seem like a festive meal.

After the tree comes down and the holiday decorations are once again stowed away for the year, the Christmas china is replaced by Moss Rose. A legacy from my mother and grandmother, with additions given to me by dear friends, this delicate rose pattern tea set is a reminder of the wonderful women in my life as well as the changing of the seasons.

Glenna: I have fond memories from my childhood and teenage years of rearranging furniture in my bedroom to feel like things were new and different, even though nothing material was new. I know my mother had done the same growing up, and she helped her daughters experience the kind of excitement that one might usually feel from buying a new piece of furniture by doing something that cost nothing but produced a similar joy. I passed on the same joy to my kids by encouraging them to change their bedrooms around as they were growing up— sometimes switching rooms to make the effect more dramatic. But when it came to shared areas of the house, my husband has never been keen on the idea of rearranging furniture! Maybe this is because he travels so much, and he appreciates coming home to the familiar. So instead of rearranging furniture, I've focused more on changing small things, like a new dried flower arrangement in the hallway or a wreath over the fireplace as the seasons change.

But truly what has had the most impact on any plan for reordering my home has been moving the number of times we've moved, as well as the places we've lived. In our twenty-seven years of marriage, our longest tenure at any one home has been six years, and we've spent two years each in four different homes overseas.

With each move, we needed to buy additional furniture because the level of provided furnishing decreased. When we moved back to the Chicago area in 2004 and bought a house, it was hugely exciting to wait for our shipment from China and then to find the perfect place for everything. Now there is only one room in the house in which I'd like to move the furniture around! And interestingly, it's the room with furniture that we bought here in the States because we had nothing for a family room. Every once in a while, I'll take a look at some of the imported decorative "stuff" from China at discount stores, and if the price is right, I'll buy a small piece—a blue and white porcelain to add to the collection I started in China—or a little porcelain Chinese child. It fulfills a desire to remind myself of Asia. And it's so much easier than moving around a huge Chinese cabinet!

Tara: One of my favorite rituals each spring is the arrival of the window boxes. Sometime between

Mother's Day and Memorial Day I make my annual pilgrimage to the nursery to buy annuals. I pull out the green boxes and decide which windows will be adorned this season—should I do upstairs and downstairs windows? Maybe a box outside the kitchen window this year? The real thrill is walking into the nursery to choose the flowers. If my son comes with me, he gets to choose the color for the flowers—they can be all red, pink, white, etc. or mixed. I love all impatiens and those will fill the shady boxes out front. How many green vines and fuzzy fillers will I choose? This is a joy for me from start to finish. Once they are in, I enjoy watering them all season long—and watching them grow. There is, of course, the sadder ritual in October of taking them down. I always do this before our fall weekend trip to the cabin. I toss all of the flowers into garden bags and pack away the boxes until next season. The window boxes really mark the change of seasons for me.

Linda: Reordering for me is more spontaneous and seems to happen when a single item breaks and needs replacing or when I see something in the store that I love and imagine that it would look great in my home. When trying to replace the broken item (let's say a spice rack), I'll notice something needs to be thrown away or cleaned or rearranged. Sometimes this snowballs into a full-blown kitchen cleaning and rearranging, but it is very serendipitous. While shopping I might see beautiful decorative pillows that would look great in my living room. If I make the purchase, it often causes me to look more carefully at the couch, and then the rug, the end tables, etc. Next thing I know I'm cleaning and rearranging the whole living room. After events like this, it gives me a lift inside and a sense of pride in my home. My home feels fresh and cozy again and I feel like showing it off by having someone over for dessert.

Kristy: For me, when my surroundings are less cluttered, and I can SEE freshness, I am better able to do the work God is calling me to do. Reordering and renewing for me is expressed through my creating peace and fun in my environment. I reorder seasonally, in general, with decorations up from the basement, a new set of dishes for the warmer months, a different family scrapbook on the coffee table for viewing, and of course, deep cleaning.

As we prepare for another move, after almost five years in this amazing city and large home, reordering requires much thought and emotional energy (and freedom) to let go of things and to better organize the information and "sweet memories" in the form of samples. There is freedom in downsizing, and it feels good to think about what I am ready to release.

Rituals of Renewal

- Change your bed-coverings with the seasons.
- Make a shopping list for yard sales.
- Visit the paint section of your local home improvement store for color ideas.
- Replace the pillows on your couch.
- Browse decorating magazines for inspiration.
- Designate one room a month for re-ordering.
- Switch dinner dishes in the spring and fall.
- Collect art postcards for the inside of your cabinets.
- Set a pretty table for meals ahead of time.

- ❀ Keep a vase of flowers on your dining room table.
- ❀ Designate one place for family photographs that are often updated.
- ❀ Wash the windows twice a year.
- ❀ Discover the resale shops in your area.
- ❀ Take a Saturday to scour a flea market.
- ❀ Replace your placemats and napkins.
- ❀ Serve soup in a tureen.
- ❀ Keep fast paced, fun CDs in the kitchen while you're cooking and cleaning.
- ❀ Make something new in the kitchen each week.

Rest . . . Now that's something I would like a little more of around here. Let me just finish one more thing. Refreshment . . . I hope that doesn't mean bright red punch and stale cookies again, such a disappointment. Recreation . . . I think you're supposed to go outside to get that, but it's just too cold. Could somebody tell me what's the big deal about slowing down?

Chapter Seven

Rest and Recreation

Don't you wish there really were "Restrooms" available where you could stop and take a nap, have a cup of tea, or get a shoulder massage in between your errands? Or "Rest Areas" on the highways that offered spa treatments paid for by state taxes or local highway departments? Why does rest seem so elusive or something that you need to get sick to be able to partake of without guilt?

My mother used to quote the famous line, "Man may work from sun to sun, but woman's work is never done," to explain why she never sat down during the day. Being the mom myself now, I totally get that. Even on those days of great satisfaction when all the items get crossed off the long to-do list, the clothes we are wearing, the dishes we are eating off of, the silent intake of e-mails are all piling up work for the very near future. How then can we rest?

What Would Jesus Do?

While Jesus may not be the first person we think of when it comes to good self-care (although He was the one who said, "Love One Another as You Love *Yourself*"), He gave us a great example to follow of knowing when to take a break. "Yet the news about him spread all the more, so that crowds of people came to hear him, and to be healed of their sicknesses. But Jesus *often* withdrew to lonely places and prayed" (Luke 5:15-16, emphasis added).

He also urged us to "Come to me, all you who are weary and burdened, and I will give you rest. Take my yoke upon you and learn from me, for I am gentle and humble in heart, and you will find rest for your souls. For my yoke is easy and my burden is light." (Matt. 11:28.) I like *The Message* version of this verse as well: "Are you tired? Worn out? Burned out on religion? Come to me. Get away with me and you'll recover your life. I'll show you how to take a real rest. Walk with me and work with me—watch how I do it. Learn the unforced rhythms of grace. I won't lay anything heavy or ill-fitting on you. Keep company with me and you'll learn to live freely and lightly."

What an invitation! I think I'll RSVP to that one. If Jesus could walk away from healing the sick, preaching to the multitudes, casting out demons to find rest for Himself, it makes it easier for me to clear a morning. But let's start with the night before.

Good Night, Sleep Tight
(and don't let the bed bugs bite!)

My husband dislikes the need for sleep because he hates to miss anything! I, on the other hand, love to crawl under the sheets repeating "Thank You, Thank You" out loud. I am so grateful to get into bed. While we all have heard about the importance of getting a good night's sleep, new brain research has shown that it isn't just a nice idea but essential to repairing and restoring essential body systems. Sounds like a rhythm of renewal to me!

In chapter five, a bedtime ritual was described that can enhance entering into sleep. A good mattress helps too, supportive pillows, comfortable sleeping clothes, white noise, right room temperature, and a regular schedule for sleeping, even on weekends.

For some women, hormonal fluctuations can wreak havoc on their sleep patterns. If good sleep is eluding you and none of the above helps, talk to your health care professional about sleep supplements. If you enjoy a cup of tea, try an herbal tea such as Celestial Seasonings' Sleepytime Tea a couple of hours before bed.

Nap Therapy

I once read about "napatoriums," indoor napping rooms in public places. What a great concept! No more sneaking around to catch a few quick winks. Every few months a "pro-nap" article turns up in the media, and I always feel affirmed in my need to take a break in the day.

Mediterranean cultures have no problem with this. I fondly remember afternoons during my summer in Italy with a short-term mission group. Shops were closed, curtains were shut, and the whole culture seemed to take a nap between one and four. If we were having a noon meal at someone's home, they would actually point the way to the sleeping area after lunch. Sigh!

My experience has shown repeatedly that twenty minutes in the afternoon can buy two hours in the evening. Without a nap, I fade fast. Fifteen to twenty minutes is enough time to get into the alpha brain waves that can restore energy and help you feel refreshed and alert. Any longer nap takes you into a different sleep rhythm, which is harder to come out of.

A comfortable place, a light blanket, and a kitchen timer are all you need to provide a quick rest for mind and body. If you have small children, rest when they do. If you are in an office, see if you can close your door for that short period to rest. I have pulled into a parking lot, found a safe looking place, set the alarm on my cell phone and reclined the seat. Naps are especially helpful during long trips or a day of to-do's on the road. If you're not convinced, try fitting a nap in for a week and see the results!

Remembering the Sabbath

Right up there in God's Top Ten list along with the major offenders is the fourth commandment: "Remember the Sabbath to keep it holy" (Exod. 20:8). I recently heard a speaker at a women's conference say that this was probably the most ignored commandment. It is easy to dismiss this one as "cultural" or so "subject to interpretation" that we miss it altogether.

Growing up in a small Midwest town, I have clear memories of the clacking tongues, including my mom's, when "Edna" dared to hang out her wash on warm Sunday afternoons. "Surely she could find another time to do this" was the word on the street.

Everyone knew that Sundays were not for laundry but for church and for big dinners with extended family followed by "Sunday drives." Looking back, it doesn't sound like much of a Sabbath for the moms who prepared the feasts, but my brothers and I have fond memories of driving to watch cows get milked at the local country dairy, visiting the closest state park, or walking through historic Nauvoo, Illinois.

My husband and I also remember traveling the East Coast in the 1970's shortly after we were married. Back then it was hard to find any stores open on Sunday except drug stores because of what are known as "Blue Laws," which were instituted in 1617 to help people "Remember the Sabbath." Although most of these statutes have been repealed, many states prohibit car sales on Sundays, which is a leftover from these laws.

So how does a busy, tightly scheduled woman of the twenty-first century "Remember the Sabbath"? By choosing to do so and finding a model that works for each season of her life.

Creating Space for Rest

Jesus was all over the Pharisees for getting too literal about keeping the Sabbath, and that is not my intent. The purpose of the day seems to be to rest from work. Does that mean no food preparation? No shopping? No soccer games? Maybe it depends on your definition of what is restful. Like so many other principles, one size does not fit all. Even with Orthodox Jewish women who are really good at keeping Sabbath, there are variations on what that means.

According to Wayne Muller's book, *Sabbath, Finding Rest, Renewal and Delight In Our Busy Lives:*

> In the relentless busyness of modern life, we have lost the rhythm between work and rest. While many of us are tremendously weary, we have come to associate tremendous guilt and shame with taking time to rest. Sabbath gives us permission; it commands us to stop.

For me, Sabbath involves making a choice to change the pace. After coming home from church on Sunday, I usually do nothing. That's my way of getting restored. No socializing, no housework, no meeting, and I mostly stay off the phone and the computer. Instead, I enjoy a longer prayer time with God, read the papers from the week since they are always piled up, take a nap, a walk, or both, read something fun, and occasionally watch TV.

I could never have done that when my kids were little but do wish I had done less busy work and planned more restorative family times. A full afternoon of quiet rest would drive my husband and maybe some of you crazy. Last Sunday he was also taking a Sabbath, but he was outside doing yard work and cleaning up his desk because *that* was restorative to him!

When we delight ourselves in the Sabbath, our life takes on a rhythm quality: six days of work followed by a day of rest; the rhythm of sunrise to sunset, providing a structure for stopping and remembering, rejoicing and celebrating.

What do we stop doing? Whatever it is that we define as work. That might mean nixing working on the computer, running errands, taking a break from studying, not doing chores. And then maybe not! It depends on what feels like work to you.

During this season of my life, I'm trying to stay in the moment; that is, avoiding multi-tasking and looking for the beauty in life. Seems simple, but it's so easy to slip into the 'productive' mode.

How to Define What's Restful

Answering these questions might help you sort out whether or not an activity fits the spirit of the Sabbath.

Is this (whatever you're thinking about) life-giving? My coaching clients can usually see this question coming because I ask it all the time. By that I mean, does it add to or take away from my sense of balance, order, centering in Christ?

Can this be simplified? Is there an easier way to accomplish this task? Good question to ask about food preparation!

Is there an alternative day or time this could be done? Can I make the call later in the week? Run by the store another time? Find that document on Monday?

Where can I "enjoy the moment" in this?

Do I feel God's presence and blessing?

Muller again points out, "The Sabbath does not require us to leave home, change jobs, go on retreat or leave the world of ordinary life. We do not have to change clothes or purchase any expensive spiritual equipment." God's plan for rest is designed for us all.

Recreation

I have always been intrigued by the word *creation* tucked in the word *recreation*.

The dictionary definition of *recreation* certainly classifies it as a rhythm of renewal: "refreshment of spirits and strength after work."

If you're like me, and your first word association to *recreation* is something like "badminton" (one of the few sports I enjoy), or "rec room" or even more generic, "rec center," stick around and see that there is so much more to this concept.

The *Message* translation of Ecclesiastes 5:18-20 gives us a picture of the enjoyment of life God intends for us to experience:

> After looking at the way things are on this earth, here's what I've decided is the best way to live: Take care of yourself, have a good time, and make the most of whatever job you have for as long as God gives you life. And that's about it. That's the human lot. Yes, we should make the most of what God gives, both the bounty and the capacity to enjoy it, accepting what's given and delighting in the work. It's God's gift! God deals out joy in the present, the now. It's useless to brood over how long we might live.

Recreation is part of that enjoyment of life!

For some of us, recreation will take the form of sports, playing for the love of the game, not the calories burned. Recreation can also look like a hobby: Dancing, scrapbooking, gardening, birding, genealogy, reading, stargazing, playing an instrument, cooking, and jewelry making are just a few of the hobbies that bring renewal to many women.

My husband, Tom, is an avid biker and loves using it as his main means of transportation. I, on the other hand, enjoy riding a bike occasionally. Usually once every summer we go on a long bike ride along the shores of the lake from the north end of Chicago to the south end. For me, it's exhausting, yet exhilarating and one of the most enjoyable days in the year.

Another of my favorite forms of fun is to browse used library book sales. I love to pick up extra copies of my favorites for lending, find an "old friend" book that has gone out of print, or discover a cookbook I once owned. Coming home with a bag full is an invitation to curl up and peruse the pile—another form of recreation!

Renewing our spirits and our bodies in both rest and recreation is a lifelong task. Like the pool waiting for us on a hot summer day, we can jump in anytime!

Response

Do you have a priority for rest in your life?

How would you describe your sleep habits?

What is does your Sabbath observance look like?

What would you like it to look like?

Does regular recreation have a place in your schedule?

The Small Group Speaks

Glenna: When I was growing up, my parents were fairly strict about what we could and couldn't do on Sunday; however, they felt they were being incredibly lenient compared with their own childhood experiences. We definitely kept the Sabbath by going to church every Sunday because my dad was a pastor, but our Sundays really started on Saturday night, when we took long baths and had our hair curled for the next day. We also couldn't do anything Saturday night that might keep us from being well prepared for church on Sunday, so no late nights. On Sunday morning, we weren't allowed to read the comics from the paper before church; that was worldly and therefore didn't prepare our hearts for worship. And if any music was played in the house, it had to be Christian music, and so on. I love and appreciate all that I experienced growing up and wish we had done more of the same as we raised our children. But these are the things now—with kids mostly gone from home—that constitute my Sabbath-keeping. I play worship music at other times, but I make it a point to do so on Sunday mornings as I get ready for church as a way of preparing spiritually. To rest on the Sabbath, there are two main things I do: I don't do any laundry until after 5 P.M. on Sunday and stay off my computer until 5 P.M. I don't check e-mail or *Google* anything or scan the news web site, which is almost like functioning without my right hand! It's not a huge sacrifice, but I'm always quite aware of this choice, and it helps me to more keenly appreciate that my life is not my own. I also don't cook a regular meal on Sunday. Lunch is fend-for-yourself, and when all the kids were home, we kept a custom for a while of having cheese, apples, and popcorn together in the evening while watching something fun on TV.

Deb: When my children were babies and toddlers, I made sure to carve out quiet time in the middle of the day. This was as much for my sake as for theirs, and it was essential to my mental health. For two hours, everyone had to go to their rooms and *leave me alone.* I planned this for the youngest one's naptime, so the baby would sleep. I would read to the toddlers and they would sleep. Older children were to stay quietly in their rooms, reading or playing with building blocks or listening to music, but they were not to disturb me. It wasn't a punishment; it was part of the daily routine. Older children appreciated having some time when they were guaranteed peace without babies knocking down their castles. I even unplugged the phone. This daily time out was essential for keeping my sanity when the number of children at home reached six, and home schooling meant they were always present! Funny, as they got older, our institution of Quiet Time vanished. The demands of older children are no less pressing, but they take different forms. My need for rest is still present, but I haven't figured out what it looks like at this stage of life. I still have two teens at home, with meals and laundry to do, shuttle service to provide, and lessons to plan. I have four young adults away in college with all of their long-distance schedules and concerns. I teach college classes, which means preparing for those classes, and I am working towards a graduate degree, which requires study time as well as class time for me. If you define rest, Genesis-style, as ceasing from usual activity, my ideal rest would be a week at a beach resort without any meals to prepare or needs to meet.

Kristy: Going to bed is generally my favorite time of day, other than the sweet moments with my family that I love so much. I go to sleep earlier now than I used to and like to be up in the morning before the kids for quiet time with God. I love fast walks, but not so much when I have a long list of things to do. In the evening, I confess that I find television more relaxing than reading, needing some time to "chill" before falling asleep. Journaling every once in awhile is also restful and restorative for me, as well as reading and sometimes taking notes on a good book. I enjoy making lists, as I feel more satisfied when I can cross off what has been accomplished during the day, week, or however long it takes. Then, you know I love to scrapbook, make crafts, and decorate. I'm not big on spending money on manicures or massages but enjoy going to a good restaurant by myself for a few hours in an afternoon—to read and journal without disruption.

Tara: Sabbath means that as a family we go to church together. With a preschooler and a baby this does not always mean participating in the whole service! But it usually means we are participating in worship, communion, and in a good week the sermon as well. Getting the kids ready and getting out the door can be work, but it helps keep us centered on God and connected to our church community. We usually have the rest of the day free and try to do something as a family—a trip to the park or walking through the forest preserve are favorites. As our kids become more mature and can separate more easily, I expect church will be more refreshing for me as a mom. Now that the baby is starting to enjoy big brother and Dad, I am beginning to find some quiet time on Sundays to read and relax more often. I dream of solitary outings to a local coffee shop with my journal and Bible!

Rituals of Renewal

- Go shopping for comfortable sleepwear.
- Set up your own "napatorium" with a sleep mask, timer, and cotton blanket.
- Choose the best time for Sabbath observance and mark it on all your calendars.
- If you don't live alone, talk to your family or roommates about how to design a Sabbath.

- Purchase special candles to light on Sabbath evenings.
- Take a daily walk, even if it is short, to clear your mind.
- Gather books to read to relax.
- Plan a few simple meals that are easy to prepare and clean up.
- Schedule a play date with a friend for recreation.
- Choose your favorite place outdoors and go there often.
- Schedule time to renew an old hobby.
- Establish a time to end phone calls and stop checking email each evening.
- Dine like a European with long dinners full of conversation instead of hurrying on to the next thing.

I think this is the time where I'm supposed to say how renewed I feel or how much my life has changed. I don't want to just react to an idea or a new plan; I want to respond to what God is doing in ME. I think I need to go back and take a look at a few sections again. Actually, I'll probably have a lot of reactions.

Chapter Eight

Putting the 'Action' Into 'Reaction'

I was a teenager when the musical, *Godspell,* debuted. My favorite song from this innovative look at the life and person of Jesus was "Day by Day." I belted along with the soundtrack my desire to "see thee more clearly, follow thee more nearly, love thee more dearly . . . day by day." It was the most authentic form of prayer I could offer in response to God touching me in a new way through that show.

When we sense God inviting us to more of the abundant life, like any other invitation, a response is required. Imagine arriving at a banquet in your honor. The decorations are creative, the flowers gorgeous, and the fragrance of dinner tantalizing. Standing at the doorway and admiring the array is a pleasant experience, but walking in, sitting down, and partaking of the banquet is a response.

This book is your invitation to more of all that God has planned for you. You may be stepping backwards, thinking, "I can't do all that!" God knows what you are able to do in each season of life and will show you what kind of response to this book fits right now. Maybe you're good at Bible study but the closets are out of control. Some of you will easily be able to organize your household rhythms but get stuck creating a prayer list.

As women we are good at hearing with the heart. We have often heard God speak our name in the most odd places. The shower? The car? During the night? It is an old tactic of His and it still works quite well. Take a moment right now and ask God how He wants to use this book in your life, where is your place to start.

God usually starts with "I love you" and when He has our attention, He lets us in on how we can experience more of His love. When Jesus said He came so that we could have abundant life that included this life! We plan special events for those we love and in His love, God's plans for us are above and beyond anything we can imagine. If we don't ever stop to listen, He can't tell us what His great plans are.

As I stated in the beginning, we are all on a spiritual journey. Renewal is about letting God take you to the next place. Some of you have been on this journey for a long time and sometimes wonder if there is anything new to see. Some of you are in such a hurry to get to the next place that you are missing out on the finer points of the trip. Some of you aren't even sure if you've signed up yet. You can be sure *today* by committing your life to the one who knows you the best, the one who died for your sins, who came to bring you new life for the rest of your life, Jesus.

Renewal comes in the midst of your circumstances, not when they change. Wherever you are, can you stop and respond to Jesus? Accept the invitation in C. S. Lewis's *Chronicle of Narnia: The Last Battle,* "Welcome in the Lion's name. Come further up and further in."

May rhythms of renewal flow through your life!

About the Author

Since Letitia Suk's life-changing encounter with God during college, she has been introducing women to spiritual renewal. Soft-spoken yet hard-hitting, her blend of stories, humor, and the word of God challenges and inspires her audiences.

Letitia is a welcome speaker at churches of many denominations, women's retreats, interfaith events, work settings, schools, and parent organizations. Her articles on family life have appeared in many national publications. Letitia's main focus as both a speaker and writer is to encourage and equip women and offer practical tips for moving through life with grace and laughter. She speaks often of God's renewal and restoration and brings messages of hope to women of all ages.

Letitia is also a Personal Life Coach helping women find balance in each season of life and serves as a part-time chaplain at a local hospital. She and her husband, Tom, a marriage and family therapist, live in Evanston, Illinois, and they are the parents of four grown children.

Contact Letitia about speaking or coaching at:

(847) 328-2218
Letitia.Suk@gmail.com
www.LetitiaSuk.com

Bibliography

C.S. Lewis, *The Last Battle,* Harper Collins, 1984, New York, NY

Wayne Muller, *Sabbath,* Bantam Books, a division of Random House, 1999, New York, NY

Anne Ortlund, *Disciplines of the Beautiful Woman,* W Publishing Group, a division of Thomas Nelson, Inc., 1984, Nashville, TN

Edith Schaeffer, *Hidden Art of Homemaking,* Tyndale House Publishers, 1985, Carol Stream, IL